Hope

for the

Journey

Hope

for the

Journey

written by:
Father Jack Spaulding

edited and typeset by:
Mary Titone

Queenship

Publishing Company
P.O. Box 42028
Santa Barbara, CA. 93140-2028
Phone (800) 647-9882 Fax (805) 569-3274

Front Cover Photograph by: Deacon Len Zbiegien
Back Cover Photograph by: Gary Galvan
Book Jacket Design by: Gina Goodell

Library of Congress Catalog Card Number: 95-69788

Published by:
    Queenship Publishing Company
    P.O. Box 42028
    Santa Barbara, CA 93140-2028
    Phone: (800) 647-9882   Fax: (805) 569-3274

Printed in the United States of America

ISBN: 1-882972-51-1

Contents

Dedicated with love to Our Lady

INTRODUCTION

"Our hearts are made for You, oh God,
and restless will they be until they rest in You..."
St. Augustine

It seems to me the gift we are most lacking in our time is hope—real hope. What this country needs is hope. We look for hope in all the wrong places. We relinquish our great gift of hope to other people or events and often it is dashed. We hope in our government, our spouse, our children, and our parents. We hope in our church, our priests, and our sisters. No matter how good or how loving a person is, what a great personality they have or what kind of promises they make, they will often disappoint us. We place our hope in the wrong people. In God alone is our true hope; in His promises, and especially in His Son, Our Lord, Jesus Christ.

Over the past several years I have traveled around the country as a guest speaker at many retreats, conventions and Masses. In reviewing the manuscripts used while writing this book, I realized that every talk was given to help encourage and restore our hope in God. If you have attended a retreat or a Mass at which I was a speaker you may recognize some of what you are about to read. If you have not, what you will be reading is not new—but bears repeating.

I would say the contents of this book reflect what St. Paul says in his letter to the Corinthians, "...the world in its present form is passing away." *(1 Cor 7:31)* The world as we know it is passing away; the world of greed, dishonesty, lying and murder. Far from being a statement of doomsday proportion, I believe this to be a very positive proclamation of the power of God's good over evil. Yes, the world as we know it is passing away. We who choose to be people of His hope, by our attitudes and actions, assist in this 'passing.'

It is my hope that wherever you may be on your individual journey to Our Lord, *Hope for the Journey* will help bring you closer to Him.

MERCY

"But you, dear friends, build yourselves up
in your most holy faith and pray in the Holy Spirit.
Keep yourselves in God's love as you wait for the mercy
of our Lord Jesus Christ to bring you to eternal life.
Be merciful to those who doubt;
snatch others from the fire and save them;
to others show mercy, mixed with fear..."
Jude 1:20-23

Mercy is a combination of God's love, compassion, and healing. Through the Sacraments of the Church we are given the great gift of God's mercy. Before we can receive this gift, we have to be merciful ourselves. Unless we first have mercy on ourselves, we cannot receive the Lord's mercy.

How do we have mercy on ourselves? Having mercy on ourselves is very difficult. Two ways we have mercy on ourselves is by not judging ourselves, and not being critical about ourselves. We are our own worst critics. Often we base our worth on the opinions of other people, when the only opinion that really matters is the opinion of Our Lord. Based on what I have read in the Bible, when we stand before the Lord for our judgment none of our peers will be with us! It will be a one-on-one meeting. Unless we allow the Lord to show us, more and more, who we are in His eyes, we will never be merciful to ourselves.

When we are so very critical of ourselves, we are not being merciful. We basically are saying to God, "You really made a mistake with me. When You made Francis You did a great job, but with me, not so good." What we fail to realize is God does not make any mistakes. We are His children. Some of us are thin, some are pudgy, but we are all His children. When we go before God and pray, especially when we go to Him in His Blessed Sacrament, He helps us to become less critical of ourselves. We begin to see ourselves as He sees us. God made us. We are His children so we are pretty good!

Mercy begins when we start loving ourselves for who we are. There is no need to look at others and wish to be them, because we are not them. We never will be them. We are who we are. There is only one St. Francis of Assisi, that is the way it is. We cannot be St. Francis, but we can be saintly. In fact, we must be saintly here on earth if we ever want to be saints in heaven. If we do not truly love ourselves, we cannot possibly love each other. If we are not merciful to ourselves, we cannot be merciful to those around us. If we do not forgive ourselves, then how can we bestow forgiveness? The Bible says "You shall love your neighbor as yourself." *(Mk 12:31)*. Mercy on ourselves first, then mercy on each other.

If we are not merciful to others, then God cannot be merciful to us. The following is a parable about an unforgiving servant which is found in the New Testament: "...the Kingdom of heaven may be likened to a king who decided to settle accounts with his servants. When he began the accounting, a debtor was brought before him who owed him a huge amount.

Since he had no way of paying it back, his master ordered him to be sold, along with his wife, his children, and all his property, in payment of the debt. At that, the servant fell down, did him homage, and said, 'Be patient with me, and I will pay you back in full.' Moved with compassion the master of that servant let him go and forgave him the loan. When the servant had left, he found one of his fellow servants who owed him a much smaller amount. He seized him and started to choke him, demanding, 'Pay back what you owe.' Falling to his knees, his fellow servant begged him, 'Be patient with me, and I will pay you back.' But he refused. Instead, he had him put in prison until he paid back the debt. Now when his fellow servants saw what had happened, they were deeply disturbed, and went to their master and reported the whole affair. His master summoned him and said to him, 'You wicked servant! I forgave you your entire debt because you begged me to. Should you not have had pity on your fellow servant, as I had pity on you?' Then in anger his master handed him over to the torturers until he should pay back the whole debt. So will my heavenly Father do to you, unless each of you forgives his brother from his heart." *(Mt 18:23-35).*

Wow, I hate to read that! It leaves no room for grudges, no room for getting even. That means the great American ethic, 'Don't get mad, get even' cannot apply. Substitute the word mercy for forgiveness and you have, *The Father will treat you in the same way unless you are merciful to one another.* Mercy and forgiveness go hand in hand. In that parable, the servant had every right to send his fellow servant to prison. However, he had the opportunity to be merciful towards him and chose not to be. His master, seeing this, withdrew his mercy.

When we deal with each other many times we are just instead of merciful. Being merciful does not mean we let others walk all over us like we are doormats; it means sharing love, compassion, and forgiveness with one another. It is no wonder we cannot be merciful, we are so busy judging each other. I think judging ourselves and others is the way we are built. I personally have always had, and still have, difficulty with judging because I think my judgments are right. One day it hit me—nowhere in the New Testament does it say, "You can judge if your judgments are right." rather it says, "Do not judge lest you be judged." *(Mt 7:1)*. When our judgment is right it is tough to hold our tongue. For some reason we believe if we do not speak up, the wrong being done will go unnoticed. We are mistaken when that is what we think. We are all God's children. We know when we are doing wrong, no one has to point it out to us. If we live the way Our Lord wants us to live, our very lives will be judgment enough. If we try to do what God wants us to do, we will make people nervous. It is called 'quiet example.' Perhaps it would help if we pray, "Lord, heal me from my compulsive judging."

The Lord deals with us in two ways; either out of His justice, or out of His mercy. There is no doubt He wants to be merciful to us. Mercy is compassion. Compassion is suffering with someone. Justice required that it was all over for humanity, but God sent His Son who suffered and died for us. Because of that merciful act, God raised Jesus from the dead so you and I could be raised from the dead; not only our physical death, but also any of the spiritual or emotional deaths we face during our lifetime. The Lord raises us in mercy, not in justice. He acts with us in either a just manner or a merciful manner.

In which way do we wish Him to act? As sinners, there is no way we could withstand His justice. The only one who can withstand God's justice is Our Lady. She never committed any sin. Her ability to withstand God's justice was a gift from God Himself. From the very first moment of her life within her mother's womb, Mary was preserved for Jesus. She is the first one to speak to us of mercy and not of justice. She is always reaching out her hand, inviting us to come closer to her Son. Mercy is the gift Jesus wants to give us. Fortunately, our innocence is restored through His mercy, through our baptism and through the Sacrament of Reconciliation. God's mercy is found in every Sacrament of the Church. When we are arrogant and feel we do not need His Sacraments, what we are doing is calling down His justice and preventing His mercy from healing us.

Mercy is something God always wants to give us. It is a great gift in the conversion of our hearts. If we have not experienced God's mercy it may be because we are still too overcome with our judgments. Our judgments may be right, but what good are they? They hurt us and make us feel terrible inside. They do not do anything positive. When we refuse to be merciful to each other, God cannot be merciful to us. We block His mercy.

There are other ways, in addition to ceasing judgment, that we can be merciful to each other. We are merciful when we do not gossip or spread rumors. If we would listen to ourselves talk, we would find that nearly eighty percent of what we say does not need to be said, as it is talk about someone else. There is no such thing as *constructive* criticism. We are not *constructed*, we are loved into being. There is an old saying: If you cannot say anything nice, do not say anything at all. Just stop talking about others. Scripture encourages us to share with each other when we are together, however we must keep in mind Scripture also says, "Remove the wooden beam from your eye first; then you will see clearly to remove the splinter from your brother's eye." *(Mt 7:5)*. We are merciful when we hold no grudges and seek no revenge. We are merciful when we stop forcing religion on each other; when we let God be God and simply, quietly, just do what we know we have to do. What is it we know we have to do? Put God at the center of our lives. That is the Will of God for us. There you are, it really is simple. It is not easy, but it is simple.

I believe if we focus on Jesus and our relationship with Him, we will have enough to do for the rest of our lives without looking at each other. We will be too busy to judge. When we focus on Jesus, we allow Him to show us what He wants to heal and strengthen within us. As we allow this to happen it is amazing how He uses us to touch other people. We begin to see others the way Jesus sees them. We begin to have mercy on others and His mercy flows through us.

Mercy on ourselves. Mercy on each other. Mercy on God. Having mercy on God is the hardest to do, yet the easiest to explain. Very simply put, having mercy on God means doing what He asks. He asks us to love Him with all of our heart, all of our soul, all of our mind, and all of our strength. He asks us to love our neighbors as ourselves, to keep His commandments, to try to be as perfect as a human can be, and to try as best we can to follow what He asks.

So often we are not merciful to Him. We are disrespectful, begrudging Him everything. The best way we can be merciful is to be obedient to Him, keep the commandments. This is not news to us. "Seek first the Kingdom of God and His righteousness, and all these things will be given you besides." *(Mt 6:33)*. "Do to others whatever you would have them do to you. This is the law and the prophets." *(Mt 7:12)*. Keeping the commandments is basic. In what other ways are we obedient to Him? One way is through our vocation. If marriage is your vocation, then really be married. "Wives, be subordinate to your husbands, as is proper in the Lord. Husbands, love your wives, and avoid any bitterness toward them." *(Col 3:18-19)*. Look for something good to say about your spouse. If you are parents, be good parents. When they are young, give your children as much example, love, and cherishing as you can. Share your faith with them. When they are older, give them your example and pray for them. If your vocation is religious life, then be the best religious you can be. Never be ashamed of being a priest or a sister. As such you are married to the Holy Spirit and are called to be a sign to the rest of the world. Do not buy into the misconception encouraged by Satan upon the religious that says when you become a priest or a sister you give up family. You have family. In fact, you have a multitude of families!

Obedience, that is our salvation. Through obedience we find mercy. If we are truly trying to be obedient, then we will not judge. We will simply live the truth. Those who do the Will of the Father live the truth, simply, without drawing attention to themselves. They do what they are asked to do. Look at Our Blessed Mother. How simply she lived. She is a great example to us. Another example is Saint Therese de Lisieux. She was a young nun living in a cloistered convent. No one, apart from her family and the others within the convent, knew her. She never left the convent. She just did what Carmelite nuns did back then, and she did it as best she could. Now she is one of the most popular saints within the Church, and is the patroness of the missions. God is never outdone in generosity. If we obey Him, that is all He needs to work with us, through us and in us.

Other people do not know when we are being obedient as it draws no attention, it is not glamorous. However, they know when we are disobedient. Obedience is saying, "yes" to the Lord. It is living in the present, asking ourselves what we are supposed to be doing right now instead of thinking about what we are going to do next. Obedience is being really present to those around us and sharing the love of Jesus with those around us. When we are truly being God's children we see Him in everyone. Of course, that takes a lot of work, a lot of giving up, and a lot of letting God simply take over our hearts, all of which equals conversion. With conversion comes obedience. With obedience comes mercy.

Being merciful is hard work. It does not come naturally to us but rather comes simply to us, supernaturally. We are selfish, proud, and conceited because of original sin. We always want control. If we hang on to that, then we will never be merciful or happy. We will be miserable people instead of joyful people.

Mercy means going the extra distance; giving the benefit of doubt; presuming the good. Mercy is a whole new way of life for us because it is in no way judgmental, it is seeing others with the eyes of Jesus. Mercy says, "I love you as you are." It means being willing to receive as well as give. Mercy has all to do with us, in our relationship with one another. Through our relationships, God's ocean of mercy is unleashed on the world. He invites us to be His hands and His voice to the world. We have no concept at all of how or why this works. We do not need to know, nor could we understand it even if it was explained to us. God asks us to pray. We cannot see how He uses that prayer and the benefit of that prayer. We do not have to see, we just have to be obedient.

Let me give you an example of how simple it is to be obedient. Obedience is doing what God asks of you. For whatever reason, the Lord called you to read this book. You are doing God's Will. It is very simple, but not often easy.

There is an analogy I like to use which shows how the ocean is like God's mercy. The ocean is constantly there; coming in and going out, inundating us, filling us, overflowing onto us. When we go into the ocean and the waves come over us, one of two things will happen; either we stand against the waves and struggle and fall, or we ride the waves and have a lot of fun. Do not stand against God's mercy. Let it flow over you, through you, in you, and then out of you to others. Do not resist it or try to hang on to it. Let God convert your heart. Mellow out spiritually. Allow God to love you. Allow Him to be merciful to you.

MARY

"My soul proclaims the greatness of the Lord
And my spirit exalts in God my Savior
For He has looked with mercy on my lowliness
and my name shall forever be exalted
For the mighty God had done great things for me
And His mercy will reach from age to age"
John Michael Talbot
Holy is His Name

The relationship between Our Lady, the Blessed Mother, and the Catholic Church sometimes is very misunderstood. In fact, many times Christians who love Jesus criticize the Catholic devotion to Our Blessed Mother. There was a time when I found this disturbing, but now I prefer to win people over to her Immaculate Heart. I prefer to help them understand her role within our faith rather than become angry with them because they do not understand.

Mary is the magnifying glass of the Lord. Think about that! You buy a magnifying glass to make things clearer and nearer. Mary is the magnifying glass of God!

Mary is a true woman, a true human being. She is real, not 'someone up there,' not a pretty, painted statue. Mary is a mother who lost her Son. She is a married woman who became a widow. She is a person who was never in the limelight. Mary is a person who simply lived her life as God asked; nothing less, but nothing more. Mary never did God any favors, she simply did what He asked. Humanly speaking there is nothing spectacular about her. That is the beautiful gift of Our Lady, she is one of us, "our tainted nature's solitary boast."

Mary gives us the perfect example through Scripture of how to be *'light to the world.'* She is the perfect example of hoping in God. She is perfectly human, which is why she is so holy. We honor her because she is our example of how to be really human.

Look at her life. First there is *'The Annunciation';* a simple little teenage Jewish girl saying her prayers and suddenly, the angel Gabriel appears saying "Hail, favored one! The Lord is with you." *(Lk 1:28).* "Do not be afraid, Mary ... The Holy Spirit will come upon you, and the power of the Most High will overshadow you. Therefore the child to be born will be called holy, the Son of God." *(Lk 1:30-35).* Imagine what emotions she was feeling! What do you mean I am pregnant? I do not know man. I am a virgin. Who and what is the 'Holy Spirit,' who is the 'Son of God?' That was the first time Mary had heard those terms. She responded very honestly by asking "How can this be?" *(Lk 1:34).* Gabriel said to Mary "... nothing will be impossible for God." *(Lk 1:37).* Mary then replied, "Behold, I am the handmaid of the Lord. May it be done to me according to your word." *(Lk 1:38).* Talk about trust! Mary is the perfect example of trusting that what the Lord said to her would be fulfilled.

Gabriel also informed Mary that her cousin Elizabeth, who was old and thought to be sterile, was six months pregnant. With this knowledge, Mary went to visit her cousin. Within the Catholic Church this is called *'The Visitation.'* The scene is so altruistic, so wonderful, but look at its' humanness. Mary said "yes" to Gabriel. Gabriel told her Elizabeth was pregnant and nothing was impossible with God. So Mary went to see Elizabeth. Why? Elizabeth would need help, but also, if Elizabeth really was six months pregnant, then there could be no doubt at all that what Gabriel said was true.

Thinking of it that way, the scene between Elizabeth and Mary is simply, magnificently human and Spirit-filled. Elizabeth greeted Mary by saying, "And how does this happen to me, that the mother of my Lord should come to me? For at the moment the sound of your greeting reached my ears, the infant in my womb leaped for joy." *(Lk 1:43-44).* Mary's song of praise was also a song of relief, "My soul proclaims the greatness of the Lord; my spirit rejoices in God my savior ... The Mighty One has done great things for me, and holy is his name." *(Lk 1:46-49).* Her faith in God was not misplaced. Elizabeth was pregnant and what Gabriel had said was true. What a gift to us to see the humanness of Mary, to be given that perfect example of truly being human, the way our Lord created us to be.

As Mary's life unfolds in Scripture we see her at *'The Presentation,'* when her Son is taken to the temple and presented to the Lord God along with a sacrificial offering. Presenting a first born son is one of the most joyful occasions for a mother and father. When Mary and Joseph went to the temple to present Jesus, Mary's faith was again tested. She was told by Simeon, an old God fearing gentleman who was present, "Behold, this child is destined for the fall and rise of many in Israel, and to be a sign that will be contradicted (and you yourself a sword will pierce) so that the thoughts of many hearts may be revealed." *(Lk 2:34-35)*. Upon hearing this Mary kept all of her pondering in her heart. Her attitude remained *"yes*, I am hopeful, Lord, because You are here."

Mary's life with Jesus progressed uneventfully and very normally as the child grew to be a man. She certainly faced the same daily trials that you and I do. It was not until the wedding feast at Cana that Jesus performed His first miracle. Jesus was at the wedding with His apostles, disciples and His mother, Mary. When Mary told Jesus they were out of wine He replied "Woman, how does your concern affect Me, My hour has not yet come." *(Jn 2:4)*. So full of faith was she, confident He would do what needed to be done, that she told the servers "Do whatever He tells you." *(Jn 2:5)*, Jesus then changed water into wine. He performed His first miracle at the request of His mother. All she needed to do was present it to Him. She did not tell Him what to do, she simply said, "They have no wine." *(Jn 2:3)*. She trusted He would do what needed to be done. The hope was there in her heart and she was not disappointed.

Mary's humanness was never as apparent as it was at the foot of the cross when the dead body of her Son was placed in her lap. She was devastated. The tears she shed were real as she undoubtedly wondered, 'Lord, God, how, why?' She did not know exactly what the Resurrection meant but she trusted implicitly in what her Son said to her, He would be resurrected in three days. She did not know how the events would unfold but she believed with all of her heart 'it would all work out' and her hope was fulfilled. Mary trusted and was confident in what the Lord said to her even when she did not know for sure what He meant. She had faith.

There is no account in Scripture that Jesus appeared individually to His mother after the Resurrection but it is my personal belief He appeared to her first. He just had to go to her to tell her He was alive and would always be there for her because she was the perfect child of God. She trusted. She had hope and faith in the Lord, and again she was not disappointed.

In the scripture Mary said, "... from now on all generations will call me blessed." *(Lk 1:48)*. On the surface that sounds like a very proud statement, but it is really one of the most humble statements that has ever been uttered by a human being. Mary simply said what was true. That is what humility is; being very honest before the Lord, knowing who He is and who we are. All generations have called her blessed because of her obedience, because of her prayer, because of her quiet example and because she said "*yes*" to God.

Prayer and quiet example, that is the way Mary lived. For 'thirty-three years' she raised Jesus. Only a few days out of those years would we call spectacular as far as Mary was concerned: the annunciation, the visitation, the birth and presentation, finding Jesus in the temple, maybe the wedding at Cana and then holy week... at most, two weeks out of 'thirty-three years!' Most of Mary's life with Jesus was spent in the ordinary time. What a wonderful example to us since we too live out the majority of our lives in the ordinary times. I suspect those ordinary times are the ones that are going to get us from here to eternity, not the spectacular times, but the ordinary times, just as with Our Lady.

Mary gave us the example every step of the way in every part of our life; ordinary, simple things. That is why we honor her, that is why we love her, that is why we are so unbelievably blessed in calling her our mother. Mary is what we hope to be: obedient, humble, persevering and joyful.

I used to think I was obedient until I started really reading in the Scriptures about Our Blessed Mother. She left me in the dust! You and I are obedient, basically, when we know where it will lead. However, often we do not even know how to obey. We say *"yes"* only when we know exactly what is the expected outcome of our actions.

We, who have grown up Christian, read the gospel of Luke with two thousand years of terminology behind us, so it is not startling to read *Son of God*. We know that is Jesus, the second person of the Blessed Trinity. We grew up with that knowledge. We are familiar with the *Holy Spirit*, the One Who loves us, Who sanctifies us and is our Counselor. We are familiar with the gifts of the Holy Spirit. Gabriel told Mary the Holy Spirit would come upon her so the holy One to be born would be called Son of God. The terms *Holy Spirit* and *Son of God* were new to Mary. She had never heard them before in the way they were spoken to her by Gabriel. Mary could very easily have continued to ask Gabriel what he was talking about but she replied instead, "Behold, I am the handmaid of the Lord. May it be done to me according to thy word." That is blind obedience. That is saying, "Yes, God, I trust you know what you are doing. If you want me to participate I will." Mary's *yes* changed the whole world and it changed her. Mary did not know where that *yes* would lead her. She believed what an angel told her. She believed all of what Jesus said, and she followed with all of her being.

If God can use Our Blessed Mother's obedience as He did, then He can also use our obedience. It is our obedience God wants. How obedient are we? Down through the ages both Our Lord and Our Lady have come to us and asked one thing: Pray. Pray, just pray. Yet we constantly want to do more, we want to do favors for God. We tell the Lord by our actions that we could pray, but boy we *really* could, and would rather, do something better or greater. How can God possibly ask us to do something else if we do not even pray as He asks?

Sometimes it is rough to pray, especially when there is no feeling of response that God is listening. Sometimes that feeling is just not there, so those of us who feel incomplete without it stop praying. Sometimes we have the attitude that says, "If I am not going to feel You, then I am not going to talk to You." We need to ask ourselves if we are in this because it makes us feel good. If we are, then bad news. When we equate prayer with immediate response we are in big trouble.

While you contemplate your prayer life I would like you to think about the following quote from Mother Theresa who said, "God does not expect me to be successful, He only expects me to be faithful." We can do that. We can be faithful in prayer. We can say, "Yes Father." It is going to be rough, we may not always like it and we will probably whine a little, Jesus expects that! Even with our whining He listens to us.

Look at Mary in the area of prayer. Look at how ordinary, how common—in the best sense of the word common—she was. Look at how she prayed. She was not always wrapped up in a state of great joy and satisfaction, but she was faithful to the gift of faith the Lord gave her. Her whole life was a prayer of *yes* to God. We can also be faithful, faithful in little things. If Jesus asked us to pray, and to do nothing else but pray, it is questionable if we would be satisfied with that; yet Mary, who was such a simple woman, was. She simply said *yes* because she trusted in God and in God's Will for her. She expected simply that God would keep His promise and save His people. She did not know how, but she knew that He would because He said so. Mary was satisfied and Our Lord Jesus, God, Our Father and the Holy Spirit used her *yes* literally to convert nations.

In Guadalupe, Mexico, Mary converted nations. In 1531 she appeared to Juan Diego, an Indian who was one of the poorest of the poor and told him to build a church there. She said to him "Am I not here, who am your mother. Are you not in the folds of my mantel and the crossing of my arms? Am I not the cause of your joy? Is there anything else that you need?" How wonderful that statement is! We need to allow Mary to take us into her arms; the same arms that held Jesus, not only as an infant but also held His dead body after He was crucified. We need to let her hold us not only in our innocence and our times of joy, but also when we are in our suffering, our passion. We need to allow Mary to hold us to her heart because her heart is Jesus. As we do that in the ordinary stuff of life, and it is not easy, we become a light to the world.

Our light, if we allow it to happen will be virtually transparent. The Lord will be able to be seen in us, in our quiet example. We should never have to tell people how we are praying or fasting or loving Jesus. If we have to say it, then we are not doing it. Paul the apostle said, I live now not I, but Jesus the Christ lives in me. "Be imitators of me, as I am of Christ." *(1Cor 11:1)*. That is it! That is what we have to do. It is not an option. It is not a grandiose thing. It is an every day decision in the ordinary times of our life, the ordinary times just like Mary's. We can follow her example of obedience, humility, perseverance and joy—the joy that comes from knowing there is a God. We need, more and more, to say *"yes"* as Mary did. If we are having trouble doing that, all we need to do is ask her for help, she knows how difficult it is.

So when we struggle, and we do sometimes, if we ask Mary to be with us, then that struggle becomes a joy because we are not alone. We are with the mother of Our Savior. Together with her we can say, very unashamedly, "My soul magnifies the Lord!"

When someone comes to me with questions who does not understand, or is struggling with, devotion to Our Blessed Mother; I first refer that person to the gospel of St. Luke. I ask if he or she is scripture based in the faith. Most of the time the answer is yes. I then ask if he or she really follows the Bible. Again, most of the time the answer is yes. I ask also if he or she has a good relationship with Jesus and the Holy Spirit, and most of the time the answer is yes.

I recommend a look at the Gospel and the beautiful account of the very first miracle Jesus ever performed, the wedding feast at Cana. For those wonderful Christian people who are Bible based this shows that Jesus will not turn Mary down, ever. Now He might turn me down, and He might turn you down, but He never says no to His mother.

If that alone does not sell people on a relationship with Our Lady, then I point out that as followers of Jesus we want to do what Jesus did, right? Of course! Jesus honored His mother. He followed the commandment *Honor thy father and thy mother*. Therefore if we are really Christians, followers of Jesus, wanting to do what Jesus did, then it is not an option; we have to honor the Blessed Mother.

If that is not persuasive enough, I suggest asking for Jesus' help to begin loving His mother as He loves her. There is no denying that true devotion to the Blessed Mother leads right to Jesus. She takes each of us by the hand and leads us to her Son.

CONVERSION

*"Holiness is not the privilege of the few,
it is the simple duty of each of us."*
Mother Theresa of Calcutta

Conversion is not something I know a lot about. I say that because conversion is a life long process and I am still on the way, as we all are. What I do know is there are two types of conversion; conversion of life and conversion of heart.

First, conversion of life, includes changing behavior. We have some control over that. We can begin working at rooting out our sins and changing our attitude about things. This part of conversion is just for starters. The real conversion is the conversion of heart, simply allowing God to be the center of our life. The only *control* we have over this conversion is to say "no" because God will never interfere with our free will. God converts our hearts, the process of which will take our entire life. There is no rush and we cannot hurry it along, we simply allow it to happen.

Both parts of conversion are important. We can not have conversion of heart without conversion of life. This takes a lot of work. It requires controlling our feelings, the way we act and our attitude. It takes trying to shape up our relationships if they need reshaping. Sometimes it may even mean changing jobs, if need be, so that God can be more at the center of our lives.

The conversion of life is not easy but it is something over which you and I have control. We can stop ourselves from doing some of the things we are doing that we know are not good for us or for the people around us. We can change our attitude, the way we react and the way we respond. We can control enough in all these areas to see a change, a change which is visable to others as well.

You are the only person that you can change, and I am the only person I can change. No one else can change us, nor can we change anyone else! It never ceases to amaze me, as I try to change a little bit of me, how much everybody else changes too. Maybe I am just getting so good that everybody else looks good, or maybe everybody else is also changing. I suspect that everybody is changing a little. Anyone who tries to take Our Lord's invitation seriously, and Our Lady's invitation seriously, knows we need to change, at least a little, in our lives. This first part of conversion actually goes on forever. We do not just change once and that is it, we change continuously.

Often the joy of change is mixed with pain. The conversion that hurts the most and that we do not have any control over is the conversion of heart. The only control we have is saying, "Lord, convert my heart. Convert it. I truly want You to be the center of my life, the God of my existence. I want You to be number one." When we say that, God takes us at our word. He starts doing what only He knows we need to have done. Then comes the pain!

There will be pain because often we need to fall apart before God can put us back together again, His way. Most of the time we do not have a clue of what needs to happen for our conversion of heart. In my experience so far, God has converted my heart in ways I did not even know needed conversion. I had not one bit of control, God did it. Sometimes I have thought, 'No, God, not that,' and I can hear Him reply, "Yes, that. That is one of the things which needs to be healed, to be taken care of, so that I can truly be the center of your life. That is what you asked for, so I am doing it." However, with faith and hope in the Lord it will be okay. We will find things we have never found before, and will experience things we never experienced before. God will ultimately take us to a depth of joy, peace, compassion, mercy and love we have never experienced before. He will speak to us in ways we have never been able to listen to before. This conversion of heart, although sometimes painful, is the greatest trip we will ever take.

In the beginning, our relationship with the Lord is much like any budding romance. When we first meet we are on our best behavior and it is sweetness and light. We are so happy. Jesus is everything and we can hardly wait to talk about Him to everybody. Then, about four or five months down the line, we are less excited and more discouraged because suddenly we do not feel so close to Him anymore. We used to say the rosary and now we can hardly say one Hail Mary.

We want to go to the church and knock on the door and ask God where He is, what happened to Him. We should go, go to the church, go before the Blessed Sacrament! When we get there, we need to ask ourselves if we are following the Lord because of the way He makes us feel or because we believe in what He said. The answer is probably a little of both. Look at what He said in the New Testament, "If anyone wishes to come after me, he must deny himself and take up his cross daily and follow me." *(Lk 9:23)*. He also said, "unless a grain of wheat falls to the ground and dies, it remains a grain of wheat; but if it dies it produces much fruit." *(Jn 12:24)*. As a true lover, God will allure us into seeing what is really important. There had to be a Good Friday before there was an Easter Sunday. Jesus had to die before He could rise from the dead. We have to grow closer to Him before He can tell us all we need to know, before He can work on what really needs to be worked on for our conversion.

The resurrected Christ is Easter Sunday. The crucified Christ is Good Friday. We cannot have one without the other. The great American Christian heresy says, "Jesus is my Lord and Savior and if I proclaim that I will never again be poor, ugly or sick." That is not what it says in the New Testament. We cannot separate Easter Sunday and Good Friday, it just does not work. Conversion of heart involves going through Good Friday to get to Easter Sunday. The Lord has explained this to us many times throughout the Scripture, however, like His apostles, we still do not understand. Maybe when we say, "Lord, I do not understand," we mean, "I cannot control this and I am upset about it."

Even if He would explain it to us, we would not understand it. It comes down to we either believe or we do not. We either trust or we do not. We have told Him we love and trust Him and have asked Him to convert our hearts. He takes us at our word. He wants to do it and since we say we want it done, it will be done. If He had to explain the entire process to us it would take forever! God has forever—on this planet we do not. When we say, "God, I do not understand this," it is very arrogant of us to expect God to come down and say, "Excuse me, of course you do not, let me explain it to you." The story of Job in the Old Testament is an excellent example of this type of arrogance.

Job was a good man who did nothing wrong and suddenly everything bad happened to him. At that time the Jewish faith perceived good and bad as signs of God's favor or disfavor. If you were sick or poor or could not have kids, it was a sign you did something wrong and until you asked God's forgiveness the situation would continue. Therefore, when everything bad started to happen to Job, his friends told him to stop sinning and to ask God's forgiveness. Job insisted he had done nothing wrong and questioned God asking Him why He was doing this to him. God said to Job, "Who is this that obscures divine plans with words of ignorance? Gird up your loins now, like a man; I will question you, and you tell me the answers! Where were you when I founded the earth? Tell me, if you have understanding. Who determined its size; do you know?" *(Jb 38:1-5)*. "Have you ever in your lifetime commanded the morning and shown the dawn its place..." *(Jb 38:12)*, "Which way to the parting of the winds, whence the east wind spreads over the earth?" *(Jb 38:24)*. "Would you refuse to acknowledge my right? Would you condemn me that you may be justified?" *(Jb 40:8)*. Job finally understood then who was God and said to Him, "I know that you can do all things, and that no purpose of yours can be hindered. I have dealt with great things that I do not understand; things too wonderful for me, which I cannot know. I had heard of you by word of mouth, but now my eye has seen you. Therefore I disown what I have said, and repent in dust and ashes." *(Jb 42)*. Job understood that God promised to take care of him. All that was required of Job was patience.

We too need to be patient. We do not understand the 'master plan' or the Master's plan. All of our prayers will be answered, although sometimes the answer is "no." It seems that God answers our prayers in three ways: yes, no, or wait. God, in His infinite wisdom, tells us, "Wait, you are not ready yet." He loves us and will take care of us if we let Him. He will give us love beyond our wildest imagination if we simply wait and let Him give it to us. He will be with us always in such an intimate way that we will never again be lonely. We need to ask ourselves if we believe that.

This whole conversion process is not something at which we need to work so hard. Some of us are trying too hard. We do not have to gain God's favor in order for Him to convert us. He wants us to stand still and let it happen. We need to listen to what God is saying and encouraging us to do. We need to truly embrace the cross of our humanness so He can heal us the way He wants to heal us. Not *fix* us, He does not *fix* anybody; He *heals* us. We are not machines, we are people. We are not fixed, we are healed. When we do not accept who we are, we block His healing. We need to ask ourselves what it is about our humanness we still need to accept, to embrace.

In order to listen to God we need to first be silent. We need to listen more and talk less. I think that is why God gave us two ears and one mouth. Of the young adults I have been associated with who really started listening to Our Lord, virtually every one of them felt called to make changes in relationships in their lives. Some also changed jobs once they realized their job was the center of their life, instead of the Lord. It seems, if we listen to the Lord, He may call us out of what we are doing because He sees we need a lot of reshaping.

Once this process of reshaping and conversion is underway, He often puts us back into the very same arena from which we were called. This can be frightening, but it is really very logical. We are returning as different people with different priorities, and the Lord may need us in that same arena to be a sign of conversion to the other people in that arena with whom we rub shoulders. Fellow workers and/or clients that come to us can see the change of life that has taken place. Because we have said yes to that change we are perfect examples that there really is a different way of living. We can be involved in business and still be good and honest, holy and happy, intelligent and exciting people. It is not necessary to be sucked dry of all our enthusiasm and morals, and all the things we know are right, just because we are involved in the business world.

Sometimes when we begin to really listen to the Lord we may wonder if, with everything that is happening to us, we are being called to be a priest or sister; especially if we have not really decided yet which way our lives needs to go. I have encountered this with many young adults who are on fire with the love of Our Lord and Our Lady. They are so enthusiastic. They want to do all kinds of good things, but do not want to do anything that Our Lord or Our Lady does not want them to do. Most of the time I simply ask them, "Did Our Lord or Our Lady ask you to be a priest or a nun?" The answer, more often than not, is "No." Then I tell them, "Do not do Them any favors, They do not want any." Those vocations are wonderful but they are not for everyone.

If everyone became a priest or a nun, then who would act as 'leaven' for the world? I can talk about conversion, I can show by the way I live that I am trying to allow the Lord to convert me, but everyone expects a priest to be converted! You are supposed to be good if you are a priest. What people do not understand is we are all supposed to be good, and it is possible to be good. That is where a lay person truly can touch far more people than I ever will. There is no doubt about it. Some people do not want anything to do with a priest or religious sister, which is why there are people lay persons can touch who I cannot. Lay people can touch them because lay people are 'in the world.' They are like everyone else in most ways. God can use intelligent, attractive, enthusiastic people with good personalities in the work place to show by their actions the way to live out what Our Lord asks.

We will be the 'salt of the earth' and the 'light to the world' as we continue the conversion of our lives and allow God to continue the conversion of our hearts.

'Conversion' is not *part* of our journey to God; it *is* our journey to Him, and He needs to be in the driver's seat!

FORGIVENESS

"Jesus, Holy Messiah, all honor is yours forever.
Jesus, Lord of Creation, be Lord of my life forever."
Michael John Poirier
Holy Messiah

Allowing Jesus to be the Lord of our lives very simply means putting Him at the center of our lives, allowing Him to be our God. This is probably the most difficult aspect of Jesus' mercy and love for us to put into perspective, because it is the most difficult to live. To put God at the center of our lives we must be able to say, "God, I am your child. I love you. Please give me the strength to allow you to love me." This requires one very, very, hard thing—forgiveness. There is no way around it; if we put the Lord at the center of our lives, then we have to forgive. When we truly allow Him to be the Lord of our lives, we automatically allow His mercy, forgiveness, and healing to saturate our very being. When we do not, we prevent that from happening.

Forgiveness is rough because we have been hurt, and many of us are still hurting. We are hurt so often. We nurture our pain, letting it grow and fester. It then becomes the lord of our life, causing even more pain, and guilt, because we know we are supposed to forgive. When we say, "I will forgive you, but I will never forget," or "I don't get mad, I get even," that is not being forgiving. Statements like these may give us momentary satisfaction, but they will also give us lasting guilt. We carry that guilt with us all the time and we have to deal with it. If we do not, it becomes the lord of our lives.

When even the sight of the person who has hurt us upsets us, how are we supposed to deal with that pain and grant forgiveness? One way, which may sound funny but it works, is to think about dragging that person—the one who has caused, and may still be causing, the most pain—up to the altar and dropping him or her under the crucifix. Then, saying to the Lord, "Jesus, you died for this slob, I didn't. You keep him/her until I can find it in my heart to forgive." If the person who is the source of our pain is really obnoxious, then carry that thought one step further. Think about shoving that person into the tabernacle. It can give great pleasure to picture the flailing arms and legs of that person as he or she is being shoved into the little gold box, then to watch the doors of the tabernacle closing after Communion. By doing this, we begin the process of forgiveness because we are asking the Lord to help us eventually *want* to forgive.

As Americans we buy into the 'all or nothing' philosophy. Forgiveness is not 'all or nothing.' Forgiveness is a process that takes time, sometimes years. I believe there are at least six steps to forgiveness:

1) Admitting we have been hurt.
2) Admitting we do not want to forgive, because we are still hurting; and giving to Jesus, either at the cross or in the tabernacle, the person who is causing our pain.
3) Asking for the grace to want to forgive the person.
4) Asking to see the person through the eyes of Jesus.

5) Forgiving — realizing the person who hurt us is also hurting.

6) Thanking God for that person in our lives; because without the occurrence of the event which caused the pain, we would not be where we are in our relationship with God.

God asks us to accept one step at a time. When we start doing that we drop our burdens where they need to be dropped, with Our Lord. With each step we receive the Lord's strength. During every Mass the tabernacle is opened so we can receive the Eucharist. Each time we receive the Lord, and give to Him the one who is causing us pain, we are strengthened. Eventually, we will be so filled with the Lord that we will be able to see that poor slob through the eyes of Jesus. Will this take a long time? Probably. Most of us were not hurt over night, and most of us will not forgive over night! The fruits of forgiveness are, however, worth all the effort put forth.

When we make Jesus the Lord of our lives, everything else falls into place. Of course this does not mean we will never have bad days when we get a speeding ticket or disagree with family or friends. Bad days are a part of life. This does mean we will be able to look at all the chaos the devil stirs and put it into perspective.

Let us ask ourselves, "Who is the Lord of my life today?" Who did we think of when we woke up this morning, and throughout the day? How did we spend most of our time today? Whether it was work, school, children, or a significant other, that became the lord of our lives today. None of these will save us or bring us eternal life. When God is not the center of our lives we are merely existing instead of really living. We exist from worry to worry, from anxiety to anxiety, relationship to relationship, and from god to god. Without Our Lord, Jesus Christ, at the center of our lives, everything falls apart. Then we spend the rest of our lives, and all of our energy, trying to put everything back together, trying to 'make it work.' What we forget is we cannot *make* anything work. We are not God. Sometimes we act like we are. We manipulate people and situations all the time, only to get discouraged when it does not work. We must work at something instead of trying to make something work.

It is God Who knows what to do. God makes everything work. He has told us, "Seek first the Kingdom of God and his righteousness, and all these things will be given you besides." *(Mt 6:33)*. So often our reply to God is, "No. That will not work. It is not practical to give up all my control." Giving up control is exactly what we do need to do. It is practical and it is possible. When we allow God to be the Lord of our lives everything falls into place. Why are we afraid? There is only one person who can give us life eternal, why do we hesitate to get close to Him? The Lord is waiting for us to let Him into our hearts. He is always ready to give us His peace, mercy, compassion, forgiveness, and love. We are the ones who are not ready, who keep ourselves closed. The reasons why we do this vary. One reason is because we believe we are not good enough to be close to God. We are not worthy. When we hear a voice inside our heads saying that, it is the devil talking. Worthiness is never a question in our relationship with God. He knows we are not *worthy*. The pivotal question is, are we *willing* to let God inside our hearts? Are we *willing* to make Him the Lord of our lives? God loves us exactly as we are today. There is no reason why we should be afraid of Him. He will never hurt us, or scare us, or demand anything from us. He simply wants to love us. When we allow Him to love us, our hearts soften and then 'change' happens.

When we give God a chance there is a change that happens in our hearts. As we let Him love us, we want to change. We then give to Him everything He wants and we let go of whatever security blanket we are holding. The great thing is He gives us back everything! God does not keep anything except our hearts. He is never outdone in generosity. If we really believe that, then we know whatever we give Him will be given back. Physically when we hang onto something with a clenched fist, our hands are not open. Although it is very scary to let go, we can not receive anything into our closed hands. It is only when our hands are open that God can fill them.

Forgiveness plays such an important role in allowing God to be the Lord of our lives. Not only must we forgive those who have hurt us, we must also seek forgiveness. Not only must we see others through Jesus' eyes, we must also see ourselves as He sees us. Through the Sacrament of Reconciliation God restores our innocence. He heals us and strengthens us. When we go to God and ask to be forgiven for our sins, He sees His Son, not our sin, and all is forgiven. He sees us through His Son because His Son died for us. This example is given to us in The Parable of the Lost Son. When the son who had gone away returns saying, "Father, I have sinned against heaven and against you. I no longer deserve to be called your son; treat me as you would treat one of your hired workers." *(Lk 15:18-19)*, the father "ordered his servants, 'Quickly bring the finest robe and put it on him; put a ring on his finger and sandals on his feet. Take the fattened calf and slaughter it. Then let us celebrate with a feast, because this son of mine was dead, and has come to life again; he was lost, and has been found.'" *(Lk 15:22-24).* The father never looked at or mentioned the sin, he rejoiced because he saw his son. *The only sin God will not forgive is the one for which we do not ask forgiveness!*

Reconciliation is the greatest sacramental gift we have received, besides the Eucharist, yet we fail to use it. When was the last time we received this healing Sacrament, and why has it been so long? I know one reason; the devil does not want us to receive the Sacrament of Reconciliation. Satan knows, better than we do, how healing this Sacrament is and does not want us to be healed. If he can keep us away from this Sacrament, then he can drag us further and further from the Lord. Therefore, he fills our heads with thoughts like, "Get real, you don't need to go to a priest. This is the nineties. Besides, the priests don't know anything." and "What you did was so bad even the Pope couldn't forgive you. Don't even bother trying." or "Ha! This same sin again?! You have done this entirely too many times. Come on, you are pushing God, He will not forgive you again." and "How could you tell that to Father so and so, what will he think?" These are all lies. *The only sin God will not forgive is the one for which we do not ask forgiveness!*

It is ridiculous when we do not want to tell the priest *everything.* What is worth holding onto? What sin do we want to take to the grave? Really, when we look at it that way, it is surprising the lines for Reconciliation are not blocks long. Let me reassure you, the grace of Holy Orders erases the memory of the priest hearing our confession. If God forgets our sins once we have confessed them, why should our priest remember them? Once our sins are absolved through the Sacrament of Reconciliation we are told to forget them. If we should not remember, why should our priest remember? There is nothing we can tell our priest that he has not already heard, has not already done, or has not thought about doing! The thought that our priest will 'think' anything, other than thanks for our willingness to be honest and to start over, is ridiculous. It is a lie perpetuated by the devil who wants us to die in our sins. Satan is very clever. He never shows us what sin really looks like until after we buy into it, because if he did, no one would sin.

Why do we want to die hanging onto our sins? Even if we are not hit by a Mack truck tomorrow, why do we want to continue to die inside? Our sins kill us, they kill our Spirit. When we do not seek forgiveness we are in effect sinning against the Holy Spirit because we are saying, "Too bad. Sorry. You died in vain for me, Jesus. Surely, this sin is unforgivable." and we die inside. Who are we kidding?! Jesus did not die so that we could be forgiven of white lies and venial sins alone. Sin is sin. Lies do not have a color, we either speak the truth or we do not. It is so arrogant to think our sins are more powerful than God's grace. It is such a waste. God does not want us to die. He wants us to live.

Sin is not something that just happens. We do not have to sin, we choose to sin. A sin is when we know something is wrong but choose to do it anyway. We should really be honest and say, "Yes, I choose to sin. I choose to do this instead of what God wants me to do. I would rather have this, than heaven." Saying that would be honest. No matter how attractive someone is, they cannot match up to heaven! No matter how much enjoyment something gives, it pales compared to heaven! We sin because we lose hope and faith in Our Lord. We do not believe the Lord will take care of us and provide for our needs. Sure, sometimes we let Him try, but when He does not answer our prayers immediately we go for a quick fix that we often regret for the rest of our lives. We feel bad and we want it fixed right away. We want to control the situation. We want instant gratification.

One example of a quick fix is abortion. Abortion is never right. In every abortion there are two deaths, the baby and the heart of the mother. Reconciliation is the gift of hope to all of us who have been sucked into the lie of the quick fix, of instant gratification. All of us have been sucked into a quick fix at some time in some way. Not one of us can look down our nose at anyone else for resorting to a quick fix.

When we sin, we choose momentary happiness over eternal happiness. Certainly there are degrees of sin, but it is either a sin or it is not. It is either truth or it is not. There is no in-between. It is black and white. Unfortunately there is no way we can be completely white all the time, and fortunately we cannot be completely black all the time. Thus, we spend our lives in a myriad shades of gray. How we resolve the truth and how we live out the truth is a shade of gray, it is not black and white. We will never be perfect. We will never be one hundred percent. On a good day, we might be fifty-fifty. God can handle our shades of gray, we often cannot. Therefore, we tear down the black and the white. We tear down the truth and create our own truth. In America there is no sin other than getting caught. Our inability to admit we are not perfect, that we make mistakes, has torn down the definitions of truth and sin in our society. If everyone is doing it, then it must not be wrong. After all, God cannot send the entire population to hell, can He? I do not want to bet on that, do you? Honestly, God does not send anyone to hell. We send ourselves. We make the choice.

Here is a story that may help explain. It is a good example of heaven and hell:

On Monday each one of us receives an invitation to a party. The invitation details where and when, and on the bottom next to RSVP 'Formal Dress Only' is written.

Tuesday I call my friend and say, "Did you get your invitation? It says formal dress! I am not going to rent a tuxedo. No way. No one is going to tell me how to dress. Who do they think they are? I have to be me! Are you going to dress formal?"

"Yes."

"Well not me." I continue, "I am going to go to the party anyway. They can't tell me what to do."

Friday rolls around, the day of the party. I dress up in my best cut-offs, T-shirt, and Birkenstocks, and go to the address on the invitation. Feeling really smug I ring the doorbell. 'Ding-Dong' sounds loudly. A moment later the host and hostess jointly greet me. They are both dressed formal to the teeth, he in his tuxedo and her in a floor length gown. Taking one look at me they say, "Hello, can we help you?"

I smile, "Yeah, I am here for the party."

"Didn't you read the invitation?" they ask.

"I did, but dressing formal just isn't me."

Graciously they open the door and let me enter. So I go in, and looking around I see all my friends dressed to kill. They look great. Suddenly, I feel out of place. No one is going to ask me to leave, but I know I have to get out. I don't fit in at all. The worst part is I made the choice. I received the same invitation as all my friends. The decision to go against the request of the host to '*do it my way*' was my own.

That is hell because we do it to ourselves! God has given us all the same invitation. We choose hell when we choose to sin. Since we cannot live the truth completely, we tear it down.

We know we are not one hundred percent. By very definition, as humans we have limits, we are finite. God knows and accepts us as we are. He made us that way and accepts us with our myriad shades of gray. Why can't we accept ourselves? Knowing we will never be one hundred percent makes God's mercy seem even more wonderful. He has given us the Sacrament of Reconciliation to help us through our shades of gray, to make us holy again. When we receive this Sacrament we admit we have many faults and failings. We admit we are sinful. The Lord then tells us to look to Him instead of concentrating on our weaknesses.

Before we told Him we were not perfect, He knew! He loves us anyway. He asks us to be honest and open with Him. He asks for our hearts, and for permission to be the center of our lives. He assures us that no matter how bleak our days may seem, He is with us and will remain with us. God is on our side. He loves us and wants to heal us, grant us forgiveness, and help us to focus on Him. The Lord says to us, "Do not look at your impurity, look at My purity. Do not look at your weakness, look at My strength. Do not look at your sinfulness, look at My holiness. Do not be overcome by your failings, allow My strength to overcome the weakness within you."

The Lord wants to console us. First, however, we have to admit we are powerless over our sins and need His consolation. The more we allow the Lord to console us, the better off we will be. The Lord will not impose His Will. He waits until we ask. As soon as we do, He forgives us, heals us, and draws us closer to Him. *The only sin He cannot forgive is the one for which we do not ask forgiveness.*

Forgiveness of others, and of ourselves, is not an option. It is a requirement if we want to get into heaven. It is a requirement if we want God to be the Lord of our lives. He wants to give us His peace and His mercy; let Him! Stop keeping Him at arms length. Do not run away from the Lord, run to Him. When we look at the crucifix we are reminded that Jesus will not run away from us, His feet are nailed. He will not turn us away, His arms are nailed open to always receive us.

Thanks be to God for making us new! Thanks be to God for the gift of His forgiveness. What we receive as a gift, we must give as a gift!

EUCHARIST

"Bread of life, our consolation;
Bread of life, our source of hope;
Bread of life, our strength and courage;
Bread of life, come make us one."

Michael John Poirier
Bread of Life

In his song about the Eucharist, *Bread of Life*, I believe Michael John Poirier has captured the essence of what the Eucharist is for us. Our Lord, in His Blessed Sacrament in the Eucharist is our consolation, our source of hope, our strength and our courage. We allow Him to be our consolation when we swallow our pride and go to Him so that He can heal us and give to us His hope, His strength and His courage. This takes time.

The last part, allowing God to make us one, takes more than just time—it also takes work. We need to work at unity within our community. One way we come together as a community is when we share the Eucharist at Mass. The Mass is a public prayer, it is not a private prayer. It is the prayer of the community who participates. When we are gathered as a community there needs to be a response. The Mass is not a monologue, and it is not a memorial service. The Mass is said in the present tense and in the first person. The words are taken directly from Scripture, "This is My body, which will be give for you; do this in memory of Me." *(Lk 22:19)*. The Mass is not a memorial service. It is the celebration and sharing of the *real* body and blood, soul and divinity, of Our Lord, Jesus Christ.

Catholicism is the only faith that takes literally the words of the Bible, the only faith that believes the Eucharist definitely is the body and blood, soul and divinity, of Jesus, as long as the outward signs of bread and wine remain. In the Bible Jesus said, "Amen, amen, I say to you, unless you eat the flesh of the Son of Man and drink his blood, you do not have life within you." *(Jn 6:53)*. Remember that beautiful story? Many of the people said in reply, "This saying is hard; who can accept it?" *(Jn 6:60)*. They then turned away from Jesus. Now if Jesus was simply saying, "No, this is really just a memorial," He would have told those who were leaving to wait, that He had really meant to say something different. Instead, Jesus turned to his apostles and asked, "Do you also want to leave?" *(Jn 6:67)*. Peter Simon answered Him saying, "Master, to whom shall we go? You have the words of eternal life." *(Jn 6:68)*.

From the very beginning of His public life, Jesus said He would nourish us. He is our food. It was not by accident Jesus was placed in a manger after He was born. He was not placed in a bed or on the ground. He was placed in a manger—the place where the animals come to eat. Jesus said to us, "For my flesh is true food, and my blood is true drink." *(Jn 6:55)*. When He said this He was not saying it symbolically. Jesus was placed in a manger to feed us. Throughout His ministry He referred to Himself as food many times. "I am the living bread that came down from heaven; whoever eats this bread will live forever; and the bread that I will give is my flesh for the life of the world." *(Jn 6:50).*

The wonderful gift we are given, the real meaning of what Jesus is saying in Scripture, is that the Eucharist is real. It is Christ. It is not a memorial or just a remembrance of something that happened. It is a wonderful gift we are given. When we enter the doors for Mass, time stands still, and we enter the timelessness of God. As far as God, Our Father, is concerned, there is no time. God is only in the present. That is why Mass is said in the present tense. The priest says, "This *is* My body. This *is* the cup of My blood." Right before our eyes Christ comes to us. The words pale as they try to capture how amazing it is to think that, not only did God become one of us through Mary, not only did He become such a part of us that He wanted also to die for us; He also becomes our food. Who would have thought of it?! No wonder the Jewish people had such a hard time taking the words of Jesus to heart. How can this be, that He would give His own flesh and blood for us? I cannot explain it, but I would die for it.

Often times when I distribute the Holy Eucharist I am brought to tears, because for whatever reason, at that particular time, the Lord lets me understand what He is allowing me to do. He is allowing me to feed His people with Himself. Sometimes when I receive the Eucharist I am also reduced to tears. To think that the Son of God, my Savior, would want to come to me as my food.

The origin of the word Eucharist is from two Greek words, Eu Charis. The direct translation is good gift. What an understatement! The Eucharist is the greatest gift that God has given to us. It is the good gift of thanksgiving. The gift of

Christ Himself, which comes from God, Our Father, and it is ours for the taking. I cannot understand why our churches are not packed every time there is a Mass. Christ is there. The Eucharist is there. It is real to us if we allow it to be. Jesus is real to us if we allow Him to be.

Thousands of people travel the world over visiting apparition sites of Our Lady. They go to look at a statue of Jesus bleeding, or a statue of Our Lady weeping or exuding oil. People travel to Fatima, Lourdes, Guadalupe, Medjugorie, Scottsdale, and many other holy places hoping for a miracle. What they sometimes forget is that the holiest of all places is where the Lord is present in His Blessed Sacrament. The real miracle happens every day, on every altar, in every Catholic church. Each time Mass is celebrated Jesus Christ comes to us in the Eucharist. I question the spirituality of people who travel from apparition site to apparition site and never go to church for daily Mass. It is a disservice to Our Lady to seek her throughout the globe and to ignore her Son in the Eucharist, to ignore her requests to return to church. The Eucharist is the miracle of all miracles. Why travel around the world looking for apparitions when, on the altar the most glorious of all miracles happens, the Lord appears daily. We are so blessed to have this gift from God. Why our churches are not packed every day is a mystery to me.

All kinds of people travel to St. Maria Goretti because of the wonderful things happening there. Many visitors call and ask, "Will the Blessed Mother appear today?" I tell them I am not sure if she will, but Jesus Christ, her Son, will appear twice. They are amazed and ask how I know. I tell them we celebrate Mass twice a day, 8:00 in the morning and 5:30 in the evening, and that He appears six times on the weekend. Their reply is, "Oh Father, be serious." I am being serious! The real miracle happens on the altar every day. Mary may be appearing somewhere, but Jesus Christ *is* appearing on the altar. Not only does He appear, He remains in the tabernacle. Every place where there is a Catholic church, Jesus Christ—the real presence of God—is there. If all Catholics truly believed that, our churches would be overflowing.

If we knew Jesus was going to appear someplace at a particular time, wouldn't we be there? Have we traveled so far off looking for miracles that we miss the real miracle that happens every day? The Eucharist is the miracle that happens. It truly exists and will continue to exist until Jesus comes again. Just before Jesus ascended to heaven He said, "And behold, I am with you always, until the end of the age." *(Mt 28:20)*. He is with us in many ways; in our Spirit and our heart, in the words of Scripture; and really in His Eucharist. Jesus is present in every Catholic church and tabernacle. He remains with us in His Blessed Sacrament.

This crazy world of ours is spinning right out of control and sometimes we spin with it. We need to stop spinning and come in to the quiet that Jesus offers us in His Blessed Sacrament. He will give us His grace and strength if we allow Him. He wants to heal, forgive and encourage us. He wants to give us consolation, hope, strength and courage. We need to go to Him and ask Him because He will not impose Himself upon us. Since we are human we probably need to ask Him repeatedly before His message will sink into our heads and our hearts. Jesus knows that and therefore remains with us as He promised He would.

Every equation has two parts. The first part of the Eucharistic equation is the real presence of Jesus; the second part is our presence. What does it mean to be really present? Jesus is really present under the species of bread and wine. It is not merely a piece of bread and a cup of wine; it is Jesus' body and blood, soul and divinity. How are we really present? I always pray that the Lord will help me to be as really present to Him as He is to me. One of the prayers I use, which says a great deal about being really present, goes like this:

> *Lord, Jesus, as I kneel before Your hidden presence, help me respond to Your graces so that I may be as really present to You, as You are to me, in the most Blessed Sacrament of Your love and mercy. Allow Your radiant presence to re-ignite the fire of Your Spirit within me, so that I may be Your Sacrament of love and mercy to all. Amen.*

We can be physically present somewhere and not really be there at all. You have certainly heard the phrase 'the lights are on, but no one is home.' That is the situation sometimes. When we do not have time to really be present to the Lord, we limit His ability to be really present to us.

Have you ever had the experience when someone comes to talk to you and you are so busy thinking about what you are going to respond that you miss what they are saying? When that happens, you are not really present because you are not listening, you are thinking about your answer. Another experience you may have had is when you meet someone who, as soon as he or she shakes your hand, is looking at someone else. That person is physically shaking your hand but the mind of that person is off somewhere. When that happens, how does that make you feel? It makes me feel very unimportant and I wonder why I even bothered shaking this person's hand. Why waste my time when it is obvious I am wasting their time.

It is so sad when that happens. No wonder we have a difficult time with the real presence of Jesus Christ in the Eucharist, most of the time we do not know what it means to be really present to each other because we are always thinking ahead. We think about the next thing we need to do, the next person we need to meet, the next event that is going to happen. Maybe that is the reason we do not always experience God. God is in the present and we are in the future. God is not in the future; it is not here yet. When the future is the present, then God will be there. God is not in the past; it is gone. God is only in the present. In the Old Testament when the Lord appeared in the burning bush and Moses asked, "When I go to the Israelites and say to them, 'The God of your fathers has sent me to you,' if they ask me 'What is his name?' what am I to tell them?" *(Ex 3:13)*, the Lord, God, did not say, "tell them 'I was' sent you," or "tell them 'I will be' sent you." He replied "I am who am." Then He added, "This is what you shall tell the Israelites: I AM sent me to you." *(Ex 3:14)*. There you have it! God is not is the past nor in the future; He is right here.

It is very tempting to look at the past and feel guilty about it or look back in longing for what was. That stymies us. Many of us live in the past. The older we get, the better the past looks. We let the past, our own or someone else's, prevent us from living in the present. Often we do not allow the people we love to live in the present because we are always reminding them of their past. Part of our human nature is the desire to live in the past. The devil wants us to live in the past, because when he can make us feel guilty about the past, or worried about the future, we will not experience God.

Those of us who are not living in the past, are probably living in the future, so it is no wonder we do not experience God. It is no wonder we are worried. The future worries us because it is unknown. When the future is the present, it is not necessarily so scary. We build it up so much. We worry about things that may never happen, things over which we have no control. What is in the future is not reality. Reality is right here, right now. This is where life happens! It is being really present in the present moment to what the Lord is calling us. It is simple. He calls us to pray and to lead by our example. We complicate it by not being really present. Are we ever really in the present, or are we in the past or the future?

It is very difficult to live in the present. Our very society says do not be present. Society tells us over and over to think about the future. The Lord tells us we do not have a future, we only have now.

There are two people who have taught me more about what it is to be really present to someone than anybody else in my entire life; Pope John Paul II and Mother Theresa of Calcutta. I had the real privilege of being in the presence of our Holy Father when he visited Phoenix in 1987. I was only with him personally for about one minute, but I felt in that one minute as if I was the only person in the world for him. He was really present to me. It was the same with Mother Theresa, whom I have had the distinct honor of being with several times. When we were together it was as if I was the only person who mattered to her. I watched her with other people and it was the same. She was really present to them. Her entire attention was placed on them. That stuck with me over the years, reminding me even more how the Lord is really present to me in the Eucharist.

It is very important for us to come to a better understanding of how to be really present to the Lord, in the present moment. We need to trust that He knows what He is doing. If we could go before Him in the Blessed Sacrament and say very simply, "Here I am, Lord. I am concerned about this, so I offer it to You. I offer me to You." we then allow Him to take care of us. We allow Him to answer our prayers instead of telling Him what we want Him to do.

How really present are you to the Lord? Answer that by using this litmus test. When you go to Mass, or go to just visit the Lord in His Blessed Sacrament, do you carry books with you? If you do, then you are not being really present to the Lord. I think a lot of people bring reading material with them because they are literally afraid to be alone with God. He might say something—give that some thought! You have probably said, at least once, "If God would just say something to me..." yet you did not want Him to really say something because He might have asked you to do something you did not want to do.

So often I see people go into the church to visit the Blessed Sacrament carrying a bible, three or more prayer books, a rosary, a couple of commentaries and a spiritual book or two. All this when they are only going to stay for ten minutes or an hour. If they were going to visit a friend, would they carry with them books about their friend and then sit across the table from their friend and read? No way! Their friend would say, "Excuse me... Hello... I'm right here. Talk to me now, read about me later."

The Lord says to us, "Here I am. Put the book down. Look at me. Talk to me. Be with me. When you are not with Me, *then* read the book to remind you of the time that you have spent with me."

The Bible is the inspired Word of God. It is a book about Jesus. Why do you need to read it when Jesus is right in front of you? Why do you need to read what He said when He wants to speak to you personally? Is it because you are afraid to be that quiet with God? Next time you come to Jesus, do not bring anything with you. Just you, that is enough. Then listen, you do not always have to be saying something to God. Listen to Him. When you are always talking you do not give Him a chance to answer you. If every time you saw your best friend you did all the talking, then what kind of relationship would you have? Your friend would think, 'Whoa, here he/she comes again. I better put on my listening ears because this is going to be it!' To have a relationship with God, it is necessary to listen to Him as often as you talk to Him. He will never ask you to do anything that is too hard. Usually He simply asks you to pray.

We all need to practice being really present, both to Jesus and to each other. The more we try, the more we begin to appreciate the Real Presence of Jesus. Really try each day. We will be surprised at how much more really present we allow ourselves to be to Jesus. Then, as we go before Him in the Blessed Sacrament, we will not need to bring books with us. Our time spent with Jesus will be one-on-one, without any barriers. There is nothing more important than allowing Jesus to be really present to us, and for us to be really present to Him.

When we focus on Jesus and what He will do for us, we will be amazed at what we are able to accomplish. We will be amazed at how peaceful, hope filled and joyful we will be. When we come to the Lord, He will be real to us and that reality will be our strength and courage when we are faced with the unreality and craziness of our world. He will give us an injection of hope, peace and joy; but it does not last long. That is why we need to come often. We have to practice being really present to Jesus because we are not perfect. We are all *practicing* Catholics, which is why we need to be close to the Eucharist. The Blessed Sacrament is there to remind us that Jesus is our Bread of Life. He is our food. He is not only to be adored in His Blessed Sacrament, but He is to be received within us as our spiritual food.

We who receive the Bread of Life become, in a very real sense, the Bread of Life for others. Remember the old expression, you are what you eat? It is true! It does not mean we are Jesus, it means the more we allow Him to come to us in His Eucharist, the more we live now; not us, but Christ lives in us. St. Paul says this so beautifully in his letter to the Galatians, "yet I live, no longer I, but Christ lives in me." *(Ga 2:20)*.

I encourage you to use the prayer mentioned earlier in this chapter when you visit the Blessed Sacrament. I think it will put you in focus with why you are there. Jesus in His Eucharist, in His Blessed Sacrament, wants to be your consolation, your hope, your courage and your strength. Without Him you are weak, which is why it is kind of ridiculous to think you only need to receive Him once a week.

Could you image how we would be if we only ate once a week? We would lose a few pounds, but we would also die.

Surely most of us feed ourselves at least twice a day, most of the time three times a day. We want to take care of our bodies so they will last for eighty years. Spiritually we feed ourselves once a week because we do not want to go to hell. That does not make sense! What kind of people are we? Look at how dumb our habits are in the area of spirituality. Jesus comes to us every day on the altar and we say, "I don't have time for that." If we truly believe Jesus is in the Eucharist, how can we possibly get by with feeding ourselves once a week? Spiritually we are starving ourselves. I do not think we really believe. For many of us the Eucharist has become just something that is there for when we want it. I am telling you now, that thought is not going to work anymore. We have to live our belief in the Real Presence of Jesus. We do that by allowing Him, first of all, to be our consolation.

Jesus wants to be our consolation in His Eucharist and in His Most Blessed Sacrament. This is a very difficult thing for us to allow to happen because to be consoled we have to admit we are hurting. There are a million reasons why we do not like to admit that. So many times we say, "Oh, I'm fine," when asked how we are doing, only it is not true. We are so hurt, and yet we do not allow others to help us because we do not want to admit we are in need. Maybe we do not even know what we need, but we are in need. It is no wonder we cannot, or will not, allow the Lord to be our consolation when we do not allow the people around us to console us. We say, "I can handle it, it's not that bad." Not that bad?! If we can say something is not that bad, then it is not that good either. Why do we want to settle for *not that good*? Why do we settle for less than the Lord wants for us? He said, very plainly,

"I came that they might have life and have it more abundantly." *(Jn 10:10)*.

Have you ever been in the position of trying to give consolation to someone who is hurting? When the person who is hurting keeps us at a distance we feel bad. We may have even said, "I don't know what I can do for this person. I want to do something, but this person is so distant. Because he/she is so hurt walls have been put up." This is exactly the same feeling Jesus has with us when we keep Him at a distance. Until we drop our barriers; until we drop our pride; until we stop wanting to be in control, Jesus cannot help us the way He wants to help us, the way we need to be helped.

What we want is not always what we need. We say to Jesus, "This is what I want. This is what I need." then when He does not answer us the way we want Him to, we leave Him. That is when we numb our pain with other gods, the god of money or power, the god of sex or drugs. Jesus is the only one who can heal us. He can take away our pain and truly console us. He knows what we need. Why do we think we can take care of it without Him? How dumb can we be?

We have Jesus, Our Savior, who has given Himself to us as our food. He is waiting for every one of us to return to Him so He can take us in His arms and heal us. The best way we can help ourselves is by admitting before the Lord we are helpless. We are powerless. We are weak. Jesus gives us that example Himself. Look at how weak He became when it was time to do the Father's Will. He said, "Abba, Father, all things are possible to you. Take this cup away from me, but not what I will but what you will." *(Mk 14:36)*. Jesus, in His humanity, realized His need for God.

When Jesus was nailed to the cross He was in agony. He bet His life on what His Father had said to Him. Belief that the Word of God would be fulfilled sustained Him. When we read in Scripture that Jesus was the *Son of God*, do we believe He was also human? His suffering was no less painful than the suffering of the two criminals crucified with Him. Jesus called to His Father for consolation. We need to do the same. If we do not go to Him, how can we expect Him to console us? How can He heal us if we do not pour out our hearts to Him?

In prayer, sometimes we hedge our bets. We pray, but we have an alternate plan for when our prayers do not work. We ask God to jump through hoops for us, or we totally ignore Him and think we can handle any and all situations we get ourselves into. What we forget is we do not know everything, in fact we hardly know anything. We need to admit that and ask Jesus to teach us. In our minds we have created Him into our image of what God should be, thus we have no idea of who He really is to us. It takes a lot of humility to go before the Lord in His Blessed Sacrament and say, very simply, "Lord, show me who You are. Give me the strength in my weakness to allow You to be the God You want to be for me, the God that You are." Humility—we do not know how to be humble. It is no wonder God cannot console us. Only people who realize they are in need, whose barriers are let down, can be consoled. We can only receive when we allow others to give.

Until each one of us learns how to receive and admit our need, we can not give. If we do not learn how to receive, then our giving is condescending. When was the last time we let someone know we needed something? Have we allowed ourselves to be seen as needy or vulnerable recently? When was the last time we let someone help us? Our Lord cannot be our consolation until we change our perspective of receiving. It is not necessarily better to give than to receive. When we say to God, "I can handle it," He says, "Okay, I will wait." God will never impose upon our free will. We cannot receive if we do not want to receive. God is waiting to give us His consolation. Why do we keep Him waiting? Why do we have to hit bottom before we ask for help?

We need to look at our relationships. If we cannot humble ourselves before others, how can we humble ourselves before God? It is prideful to think we never need anyone's help. Being on the receiving end is sometimes uncomfortable, but it is never wrong to receive. In our relationships with each other we need to first practice true humility, and then ask for help. If we need someone to pray for us, ask them to, and they will. What area of our lives is in need of consolation? Where do we need to receive? Which area of our lives do we block off from everyone, including God? Let us allow God to console us and feed us. He is there to help us realize we are not alone.

The very point of consolation is not what is said, but the fact someone is there. Often when we want to console someone and we do not know what to say, we simply give that person a hug. That is truly being consoling. Over and over, in many parts of Sacred Scripture, the Lord has said to us, "I am with you. I am here. You are not alone." We are trying to do whatever it is we are doing alone, and we are not succeeding. Opening ourselves up for consolation means admitting we need help, and cannot make it on our own. Stating our need is not a show of weakness, it is an acknowledgment that we belong to one another. Together we are the Body of Christ. We are all members of one body. If something happens to one member, the whole body hurts.

"There are many parts, yet one body. The eye cannot say to the hand, 'I do not need you,' nor again the head to the feet, 'I do not need you.' Indeed, the parts of the body that seem to be weaker are all the more necessary." *(1Cor 12:20-22)*. No wonder the body is hurting so badly, we have trouble admitting individually we are hurting. We have a lot of work to do. Look again at that area of your life that you block off and say, *"I need."* Do not mention *what* you need because you may not know. Mention only that you *need*, then look at the community and go to others and ask for help. Allow yourself to be helped by others and by the Lord.

There is a story you may have heard, it goes like this:

> A man is in his house. It is a beautiful house with a view of a nearby river. One day, the river began to rise... and rise... and rise, until it surrounded, and finally filled, his house. To keep from drowning he climbed upon his roof and began to pray, "Oh God, save me. Do not let me drown."

> Shortly afterwards a rowboat came by. The gentleman rowing offered to give the guy a ride but was told, "No, no, God is going to save me." Alone, the gentleman and his boat rowed away. Later a helicopter flew overhead. The pilot dropped a rope and pleaded with the guy to climb up, but the guy said, "No, no, God is going to save me." The river continued to rise, and the guy drowned.

When he arrived in heaven he asked God, "Why didn't you save me?" God replied, "I tried to, twice."

The point of this story is that sometimes we limit God's help by telling Him how to help us and how to console us. It is arrogant to say to the Lord, "Yes, I will allow you to console me, in this way, through this person, but not those people." That is not the way to receive. Rather we should say, "Lord, I need your help. Please help me in the best way You can, in the way You know is best for me." Whatever it is we need, we can offer it up to God and let Him work it out for us; let Him be our consolation, our source of hope; let Him give us strength and courage.

If we do not allow anyone, not even Jesus, to console us, then we feel hopeless. We give up and our hope leaves us. When that happens we need to go to Jesus, in His Blessed Sacrament, and tell Him we feel hopeless. It is not news to Him, He already knows how we feel, yet for some reason we do not tell Him! If we go to Him and say, "God, I am hopeless. This situation is hopeless." then we free ourselves because we allow God to carry the burden. Jesus said to us, "My yoke is easy and My burden light." *(Mt 11:30)*. That is not a lie. If we are carrying with us something that seems too heavy, too burdensome, then we can be sure we are carrying something God does not want us to carry.

When we are hopeless we play right into the devil's hands. Satan does not want us to hope. He wants us to look at the world and think, 'This is it, this is all there is. What you see is what you get.' Hopelessness is all consuming. In the American society, where there is instant satisfaction of virtually every need, for what is there left to hope? Everything in America is fast, or faster. People cringe when they have to mail a letter instead of faxing it. No one wants to wait for anything. What is left to anticipate in our instant society?

Paul, in his letter to the Thessalonians says, "We do not want you to be unaware, brothers, about those who have fallen asleep, so that you may not grieve like the rest, who have no hope." *(1Th 4:13)*. As Catholic Christians we believe in life everlasting. We believe there is a heaven and that Jesus is there waiting for us. We know how the story ends, Jesus wins over Satan. We know this life is not '*it*.' We know we are made for God and our permanent home is with Him. There is so much for which to hope! "Eye has not seen, and ear has not heard, and it has not entered the human heart, what God has prepared for those who love him," *(1Cor 2:9)*. Why do we buy into the hopelessness of this world? Why do we listen to everyone but Jesus?

Jesus is our hope. He will take care of us. He is waiting. Allow Him to truly touch us. Let us be open to what He wants to give us. He wants to give us more than we would ever ask for, but we need to go to Him. We need to go to Mass and receive Him as our food. He fuels us with His own body and blood in the Eucharist. Make the time to celebrate Mass. If something is essential and important to us, then there is always enough time for it.

Through the Eucharist we are given hope. How can we live in this crazy world of ours without taking advantage of the great gift of the Eucharist that is there for the taking? The Eucharist is God! He loves us so much that He wants to be intimately involved with us, He wants to be our food. It is mind boggling, and we will never totally understand it. We simply need to receive and say thank you to Jesus for loving us so much. This gift is offered to us every day. We decide whether or not to receive it. We decide whether or not to attend Mass.

If our reason for not attending Mass is because we think it is boring, then we are looking for entertainment in the wrong place. Mass is not entertainment. The crucifixion was not entertaining. If our priests are boring homilists it is probably because their spirit has been trampled due to so few people attending Mass. They need our inspiration and our prayers! We can restore their faith by being present and participating in the Mass. Imagine what kind of impact it would make on our priests to have a full church at a weekday Mass.

If our reason for not attending Mass is because we do not have time, then make time. Be strong with the Lord and do it. Let us give the example of where to find hope to those around us. Let us put our actions where our words are. We can choose to *say*, "praise Jesus," or we can *live* "praise Jesus."

If our attitude is to simply find the shortest Mass so we can get in and out quickly, then we are not doing ourselves or the Lord any good. When we go out for a good time with our friends, do we worry about time? Do we time dinner, a concert or a play when we are out with a loved one? The Eucharist is so much more than all of these, it is timeless. Why is it important what time it is? God is there! Take time to appreciate Mass. Receive the Eucharist reverently instead of carelessly. It does not matter how we receive, in our hand or on our tongue. What matters is that we receive with respect, love and devotion. It is impossible to do so if we are not *really present* during Mass. When we walk through the doors of the church on Sunday to celebrate Mass we should leave our wristwatches at home. Why should we care what time it is? God is present. His words are being preached. Time is standing still. Where do we have to go that is so important? Are we in a hurry to get home so we can sit in front of the television and watch football, or so we can bake? Sunday is the Lord's day, why begrudge Him one hour? Perhaps it would benefit us if, before Mass begins, we were to pray to the Lord saying, "Dear Jesus, help me to be as really present to You in this Liturgy as You are really present to me."

Attending Mass will get us from here to eternity because we begin experiencing eternity and the timelessness of God around the altar. During Mass we are nourished by the words and the real flesh and blood of Our Lord. When we receive the Lord in His Eucharist we are given strength and courage we could not possibly have alone, but we will not have it if we do not allow Him to give it to us.

Every day we are faced with a multitude of temptation. We do not have to sin, we choose to sin. Jesus is the Bread of Life who gives us the strength not to submit to sin. When we starve ourselves spiritually we fall into sin. The devil tempts us, but we set ourselves up by putting ourselves in the near occasion of sin. There are some things we have *complete* control over, one of which is putting ourselves in the near occasion of sin. Here are some examples: We have complete control over our sexuality; if renting a motel room leads to sleeping together outside the Sacrament of Marriage, then do not rent a room! If looking at pornography leads to impure thoughts, then do not look! We have complete control over with whom we associate. If every time we gather with a particular group of people we start talking negatively about someone, then do not gather with that group. If we must, then draw courage from Our Lord to keep still, walk away, or add positive input about the person. When someone tells a dirty joke, walk away. We know what is right and what is not, it is simply a fact.

The Lord says, "If your hand or foot causes you to sin, cut it off and throw it away. It is better to enter into life maimed or crippled than with two hands or two feet to be thrown into eternal fire. And if your eye causes you to sin, pluck it out and throw it away." *(Mt 18:8-9)*. Fortunately, He was speaking metaphorically. We know what the near occasions of sin are for us and we have the ability to distance ourselves from them. It is often hard to do so. There is no doubt that we cannot do it by ourselves. We get our strength and courage from God, the Bread of Life.

Courage is defined as 'the state or quality of mind or spirit that enables one to face danger with self-possession, confidence, and resolution; bravery.' The Lord gives us holy courage. He gives us the courage and the strength to do things we would not do on our own.

St. Thomas Moore was very courageous. The story of St. Thomas and King Henry the VIII is portrayed in the play *Man for all Seasons*. King Henry decided he wanted a divorce so he could remarry, only the Pope would not give his blessing on the marriage. Henry was getting very upset that things were not working out the way he wanted. There was a lot of opposition and Henry went to Thomas, who was well respected, asking Thomas to join forces with him. Thomas refused, telling Henry what he was doing was wrong. Henry pleaded, "Please, Thomas, join me for friendships sake. We have been friends for so long." Thomas then turned to Henry and said, "If you go to heaven for following your conscience and I go to hell for not following mine, will you join me there for friendships sake?"

The same question applies in our lives. We are playing with our souls when we bow to peer pressure to be accepted. We care too much about what other people think. We do not want to make a stand. We do not want to be uncomfortable or make others uncomfortable. We are stuck in the 'be nice syndrome,' when we should be listening to the truth. If we live the truth we will not sin. When are we going to stop listening to others and start listening to God? The more we listen to God, the more we live who we really are. If we do not stand for something, we will fall for everything.

"Everyone else is doing it," is what we are told by our peers and by society. Before buying into that line, remember misery loves company. A drunk does not want to drink alone. If someone snorts cocaine, they want you to snort it too so they do not feel so bad. When you do not drink; when you do not do drugs; when you do not misuse your sexuality; when you do not gossip; when you do not lie; when you refuse to do whatever it is everyone else is doing, you make them uncomfortable.

Think about what you need to stop doing and how you need to allow God, again, to become the source of your hope. Start listening to the truth. Use Our Lady as a model of how to give glory and honor to God by what you say and do. You know what is right. You know how to act. You choose to act differently because you do not have the strength or the courage to change. If changing your actions will make someone else uncomfortable, then tough! Your intention is not to make them uncomfortable, it is to do what you know you need to do. Be courageous enough to stop and say, "No, that is not my value."

Courage is doing something we would not normally do. I believe courage is directly proportional to the amount of time we spend with God. If we do not go to Mass, then our weakness for sin increases. We go to Mass, not because we are so darn holy, rather because we are weak without the Eucharist. We know we are setting ourselves up for a fall if we do not allow Jesus to be our strength and courage. Without the Eucharist we are up for grabs and anything can happen. With the Eucharist we are strong and have the courage to say no to sin. By saying no and living the way Jesus wants us to live, we give encouragement to those people around us who are not sure how to live.

Are we being courageous? Are we allowing the Lord Jesus, in His most Blessed Sacrament as the Bread of Life, to give us the strength we need, or are we tempting fate? How often do we read the Scripture? How often do we go to Mass or to the Blessed Sacrament? What is our daily prayer like? We need to do a lot of soul searching. If we say He is the center of our life and do not spend time with Him, then talk is cheap.

Through the Eucharist we are strong. We have the strength to do what is right, to keep from saying what is wrong, and to avoid the near occasion of sin. When we go without food, we get physically and mentally weak. We get emotionally upset because our body chemistry is off without the proper nutrition. This is simply a fact. If this is true on a physical level, then it must be true on a spiritual level. When we do not allow the Lord to feed us, we are starving ourselves. He can only be our strength and our courage when we go to Him.

We need to go to the Lord first, continually, and last. When we are sad, He is our consolation. When we have no joy, He brings us hope. When we are weak, He is our strength. When we are frightened, He is our courage. When our thoughts are scattered and we are falling apart, He puts us back together. He heals us when we need to be healed, and fills us with all that we need, when we go to Him. He will not impose His Will upon us. We decide, ourselves, whether or not to be open to the Lord and to all the incredible gifts He gives.

By going to the Lord often, you show Him you want Him to give you His peace and to pull you together. When you are upset or worried and you visit Jesus in the Blessed Sacrament it is amazing what happens. As you simply sit there, your worries dissipate. There you are, in front of God, and nothing else matters. The peace the Lord offers is present and everything falls into place. You are made whole, with God at the center of your life.

I know it is time to visit the Blessed Sacrament when I see myself become angry, judgmental or sarcastic. All of these reactions are indicators that God is not in the center anymore, something else has taken over the center of my life. Unfortunately, I see this a lot in myself. Fortunately, the Blessed Sacrament is open at St. Maria's twenty-four hours, every day.

The reason we have perpetual adoration at St. Maria Goretti's is not because we are so holy, it is because we are so weak and prone to sin. We never know when we will be tempted and need the Lord. If your church is locked and does not have perpetual adoration, that means there is no demand for it. Churches are locked because no one is in them. If people would be there, they would be open, and your priest would not have to worry about an empty church being vandalized. If you and your friends went to your priest and said, "Father, you do not have to worry, and you do not have to lock the door. Someone will always be here to keep the Lord company." your priest would be overjoyed! In the meantime, when temptation strikes and you need the Lord's strength, drive to the church anyway. Just stand there in front of the building. It is a holy place! If you stand there and say, "Jesus, I need your strength. Give me courage." He will. It is written in Scripture, "Ask and you shall receive, so that your joy may be complete." *(Jn 16:24).*

In the Tabernacle Chapel at St. Maria's there is a crystal ciborium holding many hosts, instead of one host in a monstrance. The first reason for this is so the Blessed Sacrament is visible from every angle. The second reason is the many hosts remind us of ourselves; we are the Body of Christ, here on earth, we are one. In a very real sense we, who receive the Bread of Life, become the Bread of Life for others. The third reason is to remind us that Our Lord, in His Blessed Sacrament, is not just to be adored, but He is also our food.

Although we are one, we are not all the same. There is an analogy that says the Catholic Church is like a football field. The pope, bishops and priests are the referees. As long as we stay within the boundaries of the field we are okay. Once we start to get off the field, they blow the whistle and tell us. We are all on one field. Some of us are on the five yard line while others are on the fifty yard line. Some are even in enemy territory, but they are still on the field and therefore cannot be looked down upon. Unity is not uniformity, it is realizing who we are and the basic ideas we hold as true. Each of us has a personal relationship with the Lord. He loves us individually, and as a family.

The Eucharist will make us one, but will also show us divisions. As Catholic Christians we need to pray for unity of all believers in Christ. The Lord wants *everyone* to be one. We need to be so Catholic that our example makes other Christians begin to hunger for the Eucharist. E. K. Chesterson once said, "It is not that Christianity has been tried and found wanting, it is that it has not been tried."

I believe it is not that the Catholic Church has been tried and found wanting, it is that the Catholic's within the Church are not really Catholic anymore. Either we are Catholic or we are not. We can not say, "I am Catholic, but I am pro-choice." That is a contradiction! If we are Catholic we must follow papal guidelines. If we do not, it may not make us bad people, but it does mean we are not Catholic. Be honest. All the Holy Father does is speak the truth. We may not want to hear it, and it may be difficult for us to live it, but it is the truth. It is difficult to be Catholic, that is why it is so important to receive the Eucharist and ask the Lord for the strength to live this life, if that is what He is calling us to be. When we begin living the truth, with all of its difficulties, unity will come.

If we are truly Catholic we need to know what being Catholic is about. We cannot be illiterate about our religion. We need to educate ourselves. Catholicism is rooted in Sacred Scripture. When was the last time we attended an educational class in the area of Church dogma, morality or Scripture? If it has been over two years, then we need to educate ourselves. The gift of our intellect is given by God and needs to be used. Do we know what *oneness* is? Why is there holy water at the entrance to every Church? It is the little things we probably cannot remember. Have we read anything our Holy Father, Pope John Paul II, has written? We have probably read abridged versions of his encyclicals presented by an anti-Catholic press, the excerpts in the paper. Let us read from the source. We will be surprised at what is contained in the encyclicals, read them! When someone asks us a question about the Catholic faith, can we answer it? With the Eucharist, God invites us to be one—one what? We need to look at that to see what we believe, and why we believe. Study what the Church teaches to see why it has taught the way it has for hundreds and hundreds of years. We need to be based in Scripture, and we need to allow the Eucharist to bring us together with the community.

Devotion needs to be undergirded by knowledge otherwise it becomes just fluff. With God's grace we can use our knowledge and intellect to pursue a relationship with Him. He will direct us to what we need to study. When we are secure in our knowledge we are set free, because we know what is the truth. As Catholics we need to know what is happening, what has happened, why we say what we say and why we pray what we pray. It is not enough to answer questions by saying, "We just do it, that's why." How can we allow Him to be our consolation, strength, courage and hope if we do not know anything about Him?

It is tough to be a Catholic. There are many things we need to look at and some are rougher than others. If we are Catholic, then we need to live Catholicism as best we can. Will it be one hundred percent? No, it will not. Does that mean we should not try? Absolutely not! There are going to be some things we just cannot, for whatever reason, do.

Although we cannot live it one hundred percent, we can have it as our ideal; the goal for which we are striving. We must keep trying.

One of the main reasons why people leave the Catholic Church is they do not want to follow what the Church asks. They stop trying to live the truth. The truth is black or white, there is no in-between. Our actions are either sinful or they are not. We are either being honest or we are not. It is not *'in'* to be Catholic these days, but it is *'in'* to be Christian. When someone is bothered by Catholicism it is because they know the truth and are not living it. Many disenchanted Catholics leave the Catholic Church to join non-denominational churches. They come back to me and say, "Well Father, it is the same God." I hope that is true. It is not, however, the same Holy Communion. It never has been. Among Christian churches, we Catholics believe the Eucharist is the Real Presence of Jesus, the Protestants believe it is a memorial service. Although they call it communion, it is not the Communion we receive. I hope someday it will be, but in order for that unity to take place we have to live the truth. We have to live what we believe. We cannot water our beliefs down just so someone will not feel bad.

Being Catholic is not just believing in the Real Presence of Jesus in the Eucharist. It is also saying "Amen" to the Body of Christ that is the Catholic Church. It is saying "Amen" to what the Church stands for and believes. Being a Catholic is not for wimps. If we are Catholic we do what Catholics do; we go to Mass at least once a week; we have a devotion to Our Blessed Mother, who was given to us by Jesus; we pray to her, and to the saints and ask them to pray with us and for us; we accept the teachings of the Holy Father, Pope John

Paul II; we live the truth. Unity will come from being honest and living the truth. The truth will set us free and bring us together again.

When we live Catholicism to the best of our ability we are saying, "I know this is what I need to do. Sometimes I cannot, but I know the Lord will give me the strength, forgiveness, and healing I need, so that one day I will be able to." As we go to the Eucharist, we admit our weakness, not only as individuals, but as a community. We admit we have many faults and failings. We are sinful, but the Lord tells us to look at Him instead of concentrating on our sins. When we give Him our hearts, He becomes the center of our lives and strengthens us. He gives us what we need. He is always with us in the Eucharist, and will be until He comes again in fulfillment of the Scripture.

FAITHFULNESS

"The Lord does not expect me to be successful,
He only expects me to be faithful."
Mother Theresa of Calcutta

Faithfulness means hanging in there when we want to let go and letting go when we want to hang on. It involves obedience and surrender, talking less and listening more. Historically within the Catholic Church, the faithfulness of people and their continuous prayer has helped to save us. Many who are now saints prayed for years and years without feeling consolation in their prayers. Yet they continued to pray because they knew prayer was what the Lord wanted. Faithfulness is such an important grace for us to hang on to, whether we feel like it or not. It is the most important thing, and it is what will get us to heaven. The Lord asks of us the same thing He asks of everyone, "If you love Me, you will keep My commandments." *(Jn 14:15).* "If you keep My commandments, you will remain in My love, just as I have kept My Father's commandments and remain in His love." *(Jn 15:10).*

It occurred to me that one of the things we have the most difficulty with is the commandments. Perhaps we are not looking at the commandments the way God intended us to look at them. Society has transformed the commandments into the ten suggestions and has given us permission to do whatever we want. It is arrogant of us to put aside the commandments as old-fashioned ideals that are not applicable to the 20th century. God gave us the ten commandments. He even put them in order so we would know what is most important! The commandments are like an owner's manual on how to take care of ourselves spiritually. God made us, He knows what will give us life and what will kill us. Therefore He simplified it for us. He gave us a well-defined list to follow. We are His children and He loves us. The commandments are the basic things we need to know to have life. When Moses presented the commandments to the Israelites he said, "I have set before you life and death, the blessing and the curse. Choose life, then, that you and your descendants may live, by loving the Lord, your God, heeding his voice, and holding fast to him." *(Dt 30:19-20)*. When following the commandments, the law of God, the Israelites chose life. When they did not follow, trouble ensued. It is the same for us.

The first commandment, "I, the Lord, am your God, who brought you out of the land of Egypt, that place of slavery. You shall not have other gods besides me." *(Dt 5:6-7)*, is number one because it is the most important. We need to look at this in our lives. God made us, He knows the areas where we need to be cautious. He knows we will be lost if we put anyone or anything in His place, if we follow a god who cannot save us. In the Old Testament the Book of Genesis says, "Let us make man in our own image, after our likeness." *(Gn 1:26)*, thus we began imaging and mirroring God Himself. Daily, through the television, the radio, and through movies, we are told we are god. If we believe that, we fall into Satan's trap. Then, when we die and stand before the real God instead of a mirror, we are in for a rude awakening.

There are so many things we put before God; ourselves, our spouses, our children, our finances, our careers. Who is our God? If it is God, The Father Almighty, then He has priority over all of these in our lives. Of course we can be concerned about these other things, but when they consume all of our thoughts and energy and become our be-all and end-all, then they become our god. When we put God first, we go before Him in His Blessed Sacrament and present our concerns to Him. We give to Him that which is making us crazy and ask Him to keep our hearts open to Him. If we cannot keep the first commandment, then how can we keep the second, or the third, or the fourth?

Most of us are familiar with the Prayer of St. Francis of Assisi. We might be in better shape if we paid attention to what that prayer says:

Lord, make me an instrument of your peace.
Where there is hatred, let me sow love;
where there is injury, pardon;
where there is doubt, faith;
where there is despair, hope;
where there is darkness, light;
and where there is sadness, joy.

Diving Master, grant that I may not so much seek
to be consoled as to console;
to be understood as to understand;
to be loved as to love.

For it is in giving that we receive;
it is in pardoning that we are pardoned;
and it is in dying that we are born to eternal live.

What St. Francis said is not complicated, it is simple. In this prayer he says, "I am not God, You are." As Americans many of us are preoccupied with *me*. This arrogance will kill us and send us to hell because we put ourselves in the place of God. We need to really look at this in our lives and throw ourselves on the mercy of God, asking His forgiveness for our arrogance.

Who is God? He is the One Who created us. He is the One Who redeemed us. He is the One Who saved us. Let me repeat that using the present tense: He is the One Who is creating us. He is the One Who is saving us. He is the One Who is giving us life, continually, if we let Him. Unfortunately, we do not always let Him. How do we let Him be our God? It is not easy, but it is simple. There is a real difference between easy and simple. We want easy and simple; however, living our belief that God is God and no one else is demands from us a lot of letting go, a lot of dying to ourselves and our own plans, a lot of dying to what we want and surrendering to the Will of God. This is not easy. It demands a whole new way of life for most of us. When we ask God Who He is for us what we may hear is, "My child, I am strength and hope for your journey. I am, and always will be, with you. You are not alone. I love you."

Surely we wonder sometimes why we must surrender, why it is always a case of dying, of having to listen and say, "Yes, Lord." The answer is simple, because He is God and He knows what we need to be saved. It is well known that God wants to save us. The whole point of Him sending His Son to us, who died and was raised from the dead, was so you and I could live with God forever. That is the salvation God offers us. He sent His Son to redeem the entire world by His blood. Because of that gift of redemption all of us have the opportunity to be saved. Being saved is not, however, a sure thing on our side unless we keep the commandments and try our best to be God's children. He will only save us if we want to be saved.

It is not written anywhere in Scripture that if we proclaim Jesus is our Lord and Savior we are saved. Do we *say*, "praise Jesus," or do we *live* "praise Jesus"? Saying and living do not have to be mutually exclusive, we can do both. I hope we do both. However, if we have to choose, we should keep our mouth shut and live "praise Jesus." If we never proclaimed aloud to anyone that Jesus is the Lord of our lives, would they know? Would they know we are Catholic? If we have to say it, then we are probably not living it. The Lord knows what we need to be saved. He asks us to listen to Him and to obey.

What I need to be saved is different from what you need to be saved. Every day when we wake up the Lord shows us, individually, what we need. Our lives, and all that happens to us each day, is a continuing process which includes the joys and pains of everyday life. Knowing this puts into perspective all the physical, emotional, mental, and spiritual suffering we endure. With God's help we can look upon suffering as a gift instead of a curse. When we see God in everything, even in the stuff we do not like, then we can say to Him, "Lord, I do not know exactly what is happening here but I know You love me. I know I am Your child and You want to save me. If this is part of what I need to be saved, then I say 'yes' even through my tears, my sorrow, and my pain. If this is not part of what I need to be saved, then I ask you to take it away or to use it to help someone else in their journey of salvation."

I suspect if we tried our best to accept what the Lord gives us every day we would be able to allow Him to save us faster than we believe possible. Daily acceptance, of course, also includes accepting the answers to our prayers even when the answer is "no." Since we do not know what we need to be saved, we think we know what is good for us. God says to us, "No. I love you so much that I will not let you have this which will hurt you. Each time you ask for it the answer will be no. I will instead give you something you really need, My mercy, My love, My forgiveness, and most of all My dear child, I will save you." So many people do not believe He will save them. So often we look at God as our adversary saying, "God, why are You doing this to me, or to him, or to her?" forgetting it is what is necessary for our salvation, or his salvation, or her salvation.

How faithful is God to us? He never lets us go! He comes to us every day on every altar at our beck and call. He is always there, yet never forces Himself upon us. God is faithful even when we are not because He cannot deny Himself. His very being is faithfulness to us. He is our God.

How faithful are we to Him? Of course, we could all be more faithful, however thank God for the faith we have. You are a faithful person and so am I. If you were not, you would not be reading this. We are faithful, and with the Lord's help our faith will grow. Thus we pray, "Lord I believe, help my unbelief. Help me to hang on. Help me truly to be faithful, to know in which ways I need to be faithful. Lord, help me." That prayer will be answered. God wants to help us. He is with us. He asks us to simply pray. To do our best to be faithful to what He asks of us. To offer to Him our boredom, distractions, anxiety, unfaithfulness, and all the things of which we are not proud. God can deal with all that, because we are human and imperfect, we cannot. Fortunately, God has a sense of humor! He puts up with us because He loves us. We need to let Him love us the way we are.

Faithfulness is the hardest thing we will do because it means saying no to ourselves and yes to God. It means listening to Him and the Holy Spirit as they speak to us through one another and in private prayer, through nature, through Scripture and the Sacraments. Faithfulness takes a lot patience. It is not the spectacular things we do which will get us to heaven. It is the days when things are not going well, when our car runs out of gas and the dog bites the kid and we really do not feel like praying, but we do anyway. That is faithfulness! That is what saints are made of. Most saints never thought they were doing anything spectacular during their life, they were just doing what they thought they were supposed to do.

What are we supposed to do? The answer is different for everyone. With God's help we will know what we are supposed to do. He has already laid out for us some of the things He wants us to do:

Keep the commandments;

Remain faithful;

Be close to the Lord in His Sacraments, especially the Eucharist and Reconciliation;

Be close to Him in His Blessed Sacrament;

Be close to Him in His Word, the Holy Scripture;

Be close to Him in His people;

Be close to Him in His creation;

Be close to the Lord as He dwells within us;

Simply pray and pray simply.

Will these be easy to do? No! Are they glamorous? No. Will we be recognized for doing them? Probably not. However, when we try, there is a freedom about us to which people are attracted. There is a liberation of all things because, in being faithful to God, we say to everyone that the Lord is in control, we are not. Our example attracts others who want to know why we are so joyful, what it is we have, and where can they get it. When our answer is simply "faith," they turn away, but they will come back. Faith is the only thing that really works and really lasts. I hear the Lord saying to us, "Come to me, My good and faithful servants. Enter into the Kingdom which was prepared for you from the beginning of the world. My good and faithful servants, in season and out of season, when you want to and when you do not want to, when you feel good and when you do not feel good, when you do not even want to hear the word of God let alone preach it, let alone live it; come to Me. Be faithful."

PRAYER

There is a story told of the Curé of Ars who watched an elderly gentleman come into the church around two o'clock in the afternoon. The gentleman entered the church and sat in the shadows in the very back pew. When the priest saw him he thought the gentleman was there to steal from the poor box—sometimes when there is only one person in the church it is a thought that crosses the mind. So the priest watched him from the sacristy. The gentleman stayed for about twenty minutes then got up and left. The priest breathed a sigh of relief that the church had not been robbed.

The next day, the gentleman came in again and sat in the shadows in the back of the church. This time the priest thought he was casing the joint. Just shy of half an hour later, the gentleman left. Every day for a week straight it was the same. The gentleman came, sat for awhile, and left. This worried the priest who wondered what the gentleman's intentions were.

On the eighth day, the priest walked from the sacristy to the vestibule of the church in such a way that the gentleman would not see him. From the vestibule the priest could see much clearer what the man was doing. He had no rosary in his hand. He carried no bible or prayer book. He was simply sitting there in the shadows. The priest could not understand.

Another week passed with the gentleman arriving right on schedule. Finally, the priest built up enough courage to ask the gentleman, "Sir, I do not want to interrupt what you are doing, but I would like to ask you a question. What are you doing? Are you praying?" The man replied, "No. I come in here, I sit down, I look at Jesus, and He looks at me." With a confused look the priest added, "That's all?!" "Father," the man whispered, "what else is there?"

In this story the gentleman gives the best definition of contemplative prayer I have ever heard: I look at my God and He looks at me. What else is there? Wherever there is adoration of the Blessed Sacrament we can enter, look at Jesus, and let Him look at us. If we do not know what to say, we can say nothing. Our Heavenly Father knows what we need even when we do not.

Prayer is opening our minds, our hearts and our ears to the love of the Lord, Jesus Christ. It is not a practice of convincing God to see things our way; rather it is allowing God to show us His way, allowing Him to change our hearts. God sees how we struggle, often over the wrong things. He sees how we struggle even in prayer. We turn that which is so easy, into something so difficult. Prayer should be like breathing. We do not think about breathing, we just breath. When we think about breathing, suddenly we cannot do it very well. We make ourselves crazy when we think too much. Prayer should not make us crazy, it should be the support of our lives.

There are no rules to prayer saying we must do this or we must say that. Instead of feeling like "we need to get our prayers in," we should *get into our prayers*! If there is only time to pray one Our Father, then we need to pray it with all our heart. Get into it instead of getting it in.

Our Lady has asked us to pray as if we could see her standing right in front of us. If she were, and she is, we would not rattle off our prayers like parrots and rush through them saying, "HailMaryFullOfGraceTheLordIsWithYou." After we recovered from the shock of seeing Our Lady, what we would pray would certainly sound more like, "Hail Mary... full of grace... the Lord is with you... Blessed are you among women... and blessed is the fruit of your womb, Jesus..."

When we get into our prayers, instead of getting them in, prayer becomes a way of life not just something we do. We pray all the time. Sometimes our prayer is work, sometimes it is school. Other times our prayer is taking care of someone, or sitting quietly alone. Praying the rosary or the Liturgy of the Hours may be our prayer at times, as is sitting and talking to the Lord or just looking at Him. The state of our being should be prayer. It never ceases to amaze me how little we reflect on prayer. Maybe we do not understand the whole point of prayer. The point of prayer is not to change God's mind, it is to change our hearts.

Prayer takes on all kinds of forms. Each form is a tool, and each tool is valuable. Is one tool better than another? Not at all. It depends on what we want to do. If we have to put a screw in, then we use a screwdriver, not a hammer. Prayer is a tool which is used to change our hearts in our relationship with God. One prayer is just as good as another. Saying a rosary is not better than praying privately, both are equally valuable. We need to use whichever tool works the best for us. If we have several tools, that is great! We can use all of them. However, if one tool we have been using for awhile stops working, then we need to put it on the shelf and bring out another. The tool is not an end in itself. If it is, then we are misusing it. The end result of the use of our tools, our prayers, is our relationship with God.

As practicing Catholics, we must practice praying. We are not perfect. When we think we have it down perfectly is when we need to beware. It is then that we become judgmental and criticize the way others pray. We must always remember each of us has our own set of tools. The gentleman who sat in the back of the church had the right attitude. He did not bother anyone and was no threat to anyone. He just sat in the shadows and looked at Jesus. What an example! Simply pray, pray simply.

Our Lady has asked us to pray and to never cease praying. Our prayers are useful and necessary to Our Lord and Our Lady. We do not know *how* they use them, but we must continue to believe they *are* used! That knowledge should help us get into our prayers instead of getting them in.

In our lives, we offer up prayers for many different reasons. Every prayer we pray is answered by the Lord in one of three ways; yes, no, wait. We like the answer "yes" just as much as we dislike the answer "no." However, most of time the answer we receive is "wait." Waiting is something we do not want to do. It is an answer that is often confused with no. Trusting that God knows what He is doing is difficult for us. Sometimes we think He really does not want what is best for us. An example of this is when we pray for God to heal the sick, especially those to whom we are close. Only instead of getting physically healthier, they die. We become angry because we fail to realize that the ultimate physical healing is death. As Catholic's we believe in the resurrection of the body and life everlasting. Therefore, we should not be so upset when someone dies. Yes, we should feel the loss, for the human loss is very real. Our sadness speaks of our humanness, of our love. Our faith tells us where loved ones go when they die, but our humanness suffers the loss. When we really love someone, never is the only good time to have them go. So, if never is a good time, then anytime is just as good a time. To a certain extent, all of us will go through physical pain and suffering. This is a part of being human which is unavoidable.

Sickness is not a sign of God's lack of love for us. It is a Jewish belief, not a Christian belief, that God does not want us to suffer. In the New Testament there is a story of a man who was born blind. Jesus and His disciples passed by the blind man and His disciples asked Him, "Rabbi, who sinned, this man or his parents, that he was born blind?" Jesus answered, "Neither he nor his parents sinned; it is so that the works of God might be made visible through him." *(Jn 9:1-3)*. Jesus then cured his blindness. Sickness is for the glory of God! It may be what is necessary for the salvation of the person who is sick. We do not know how God is going to save us. If we trust that He loves us, then we believe what He gives us is for our salvation.

Why don't we accept the cross the Lord gives to us? We look at everyone else's cross and want to trade because ours is too heavy. Maybe it is not too heavy; maybe we are just carrying it the wrong way. Our cross should not be endured, it should be embraced! It is our way to salvation. Each of us has a cross and our crosses are as different and as individual as we are. Embracing our cross means simply accepting it, accepting the cross of being human. We need to embrace the cross of our humanness, rather than seeing it as something we have to endure. Most of us are enduring life, not living life. The cross of being human is coming to the realization that we will never be perfect this side of heaven.

Can we still offer prayers for someone to be cured? Of course! Will God heal the sick? Sometimes. God will heal us in whatever way we need which brings us closer to Him. We should remember, however, that physical healing is not for eternity. If you or I have cancer and we are cured through prayer, we still will not leave this world alive! The Lord invites us to embrace our cross for our salvation. He asks us to accept it and to let Him help us carry it.

During an interview with Mother Theresa of Calcutta she was asked, "Mother, how do you look at the rich people? How do you look at those who have so much? Should they give all they have to the poor? Should they leave what they have to come work with you in Calcutta?" Her response was beautiful, "We need to accept. If you are born in a palace, accept living in a palace. That is what God has for you now. If you are born in poverty, accept that, live that. God has that for you now. If you have food to eat, accept that. That is God's gift to you now. If you have not enough to eat, accept that right now and then God will give you what you need."

Acceptance is so basic. If we are given much, then we should accept that and share our wealth instead of feeling guilty about it. When we accept what God gives and what He asks of us, we will stop worrying. We will no longer be anxious. Anything that tempts us to be anxious or worried we will offer to God in our prayer. It does not matter how we offer it to the Lord, which tool we use; it does matter that we simply make the offering. When something is bothering us, we need to talk to God about it and then allow Him to talk back. If we listen, then God can speak to our hearts. Worry is not going to accomplish anything. It is destructive to our health and to our Spirit. We should, and we can, replace worry with concern. Worry drives us crazy, concern drives us to our knees.

During a convocation of priests in 1991, Father Tim O'Connell of Chicago said something that really had an impact on me. I believe it applies to everyone. He said, "I have three statements for you, which I will explain: first, *get over it*; second, *get a hold of yourself*; and third, *get help*." His words were great! They sum up so much.

Get over it. Whatever it is we are worrying about in our lives is not worth being anxious over, therefore we should get over it! As we get over it God will give us the gift of joy. We really need to practice using this gift. There is no reason not to be joyful! There is no doubt we have trials and crosses in our lives, but we know how we will end up if we allow God to be the center of our lives. This earth is a lovely place, but we are only visitors here. This is only a stop on our journey which we need to enjoy as best we can. If we would begin to act as though we believed our home was Heaven, then there would be true joy within us. We would live simply, speak honestly, and our attitude would be of joy and of hope. Joy goes with *get over it*. Hope goes with *get a hold of yourself*.

Get a hold of yourself. We are not orphans. We are children of God. Not only do we know what the end is, we also know the path to get there; through the church, the Sacraments, and the Scripture. All of these are here to help us. How do we get a hold of ourselves? We look at our lives to see what is causing us grief and we deal the problem. There is so much hopelessness in the world today, being hope-filled people who look for joy and goodness in others is contagious and spreads hope. Get over it, be joyful. Get a hold of ourselves, be hopeful.

Lastly, get help. Being a 'Lone Ranger' spiritually, or in any other way, does not work. It is not Jesus and me, it is Jesus and we. Look at the New Testament. All throughout the story of the beginning of the Church we see community. When we are given what we are given by the Lord, our crosses, we cannot carry them alone. We need the support of our community. Prayer groups, either within the church or at home—the domestic church—are wonderful! Praying in a group is very important. It fills us with hope and strength. Does the group have to have twenty people? No. A group is simply two or more. Does this imply we should give up individual prayer? Absolutely not. Personal prayer is a prerequisite. When we come together as a group to pray, all we should do is pray. Discussion, interpretation, and sharing are all valid and helpful but should not take the place of prayer. When we gather to pray, please pray. Getting help spiritually through the community is a great gift. In addition, getting help spiritually as individuals, through a spiritual director, is suggested. A spiritual director is someone who has been on the spiritual journey longer than ourselves; perhaps a priest, a sister, or another lay person who is not a family member. A spouse or family member is too close and therefore prejudiced. Spiritual direction is the gift of objectivity for you and me. Certainly, we need to be comfortable with our spiritual director. Someone once said, "If I had to choose between a holy person and an intelligent person as a spiritual director I would choose the intelligent person. Holiness and intelligence are both gifts from God, but an intelligent person—if worth their salt—will be objective and not 'ooh' and 'ahh' over my spiritual experiences." To be comfortable, we must like our spiritual director and feel a need for a spiritual director. If we ask the Lord if this is the time for us to have a spiritual director, He will let us know. If it is, then we need to pray for one, as a good director is a real help and a real gift.

Get over it, get a hold of ourselves, and get help. Give to God everything which causes us anxiety or worry. When we do this we will no longer be anxious and worried. We will be joyful. In our prayer we need to present ourselves to the Lord for healing, forgiveness, and all that we need which we are not even aware we need.

Do we become distracted in our prayer? Certainly we do! At times our minds wander. When they do, we can offer our wanderings and distractions to Jesus. It is possible our distractions are the Holy Spirit asking us to offer to God the things about which we are worried. Our distractions may be what the Lord wants us to pray about. Another possibility is that our distractions are from Satan who wants us to stop praying. However, if we offer our distractions to the Lord, then they are of no use to Satan. The devil wants no part in any offering to God. When we become distracted and offer our distractions to the Lord, if they are from Satan they will go away, if they are from the Holy Spirit they will not. Whatever the origin of our distractions, we need to accept them and offer them to the Lord. What we should not do is get all upset about them during prayer and stop praying.

We should not think that if we are distracted our prayers are not good. We cannot judge what is a good prayer and what is not! Our prayers are good because they encompass who we are at the time we are praying. At that moment in prayer, that is who we are. We may be full of distractions, full of anger, or full of hurt, which is okay as long as we offer it to the Lord. Prayer allows God the opportunity to change our hearts. During our prayers there are two things we must remember; do not pray for anything we are not ready to accept, and give God the opportunity to help us.

CHILD OR BRAT?

"A saint is someone who knows God loves him
and then acts like it."
Unknown

Unless you are a saint here on earth, you are not going to be one in heaven. It is that simple. Never say, "I am no saint," because that is offensive to God. We should be saints, saints in the making. To do so we need to enjoy the journey, be excited about what God has planned for us! He has plans we have not even contemplated. He knows exactly what we need to get where we need to go. It is all part of the journey; the crosses and suffering, the joys and craziness, and the ordinariness. All of these are part of the journey to the Lord.

We all need to work at our sanctity. I imagine most people think, on their better days, that God likes them. Even so, they do not always act like it. They are probably not sure because they think God's love depends on how they are doing, only His love does not depend on anything! He loves every individual unconditionally. This uncertainty of God's love is the difference between real saints, and average people who are seldom sure of His love and are unwilling to commit to Him, to make Him the center of their lives. If we are not working on our sanctity, then we are not living up to who we are, because we are God's children.

True children are completely and totally trusting of their parents. They try as best they can to receive the love their parents offer. Being obedient and honest, giving their parents the benefit of the doubt, is second nature to them. True children do not seek to be in control.

Often we do not act like God's children, rather we act like brats. We do not trust. We are not obedient. We want everything and we want it now. If we do not get our way, then we do not want to play. We yell and scream and say things like, "Okay, God, you didn't answer my prayers so I am never going to pray again." We are brats! Sometimes we cut off our nose to spite our face. We limit what God wants to do for us because He does not do it our way. Instead of talking to God we whine and say, "Where are you? Why haven't you been talking to me?"

Can you imagine what God listens to every day?! We should give God a break and talk to Him instead of whining. You and I can talk to God, just like a child can talk to his father. We can also listen to God. A brat does not listen at all. Instead, a brat says, "Now listen, God..." Because He loves us, God does listen. The main ingredient of a brat is lack of love. A brat does not really feel loved. However, if that is the reason we act like brats, it is not good enough because God loves us unconditionally. If we forget that, all we have to do is look at the crucifix. That is how much God loves us.

You may have heard this story: Someone asked Jesus, "How much do you love me, Jesus?" He answered, "This much." He then outstretched His arms and died.

Wow! We are really loved. In this journey of ours Jesus has told us He loves us completely and is with us. He is with us always, and will be until the end of time. Until we totally believe this, we will not truly be children of God.

It is by our actions we show we are brats. We always want our own way. If we do not get our own way we throw a tantrum. When we do so, we are focusing only on ourselves and feeling sorry for ourselves. Look at a little kid who is throwing a temper tantrum. Obviously one reason to have a tantrum is to draw attention. Another reason really is to push everyone else away. Brats are not very lovable. Who wants to be around a little kid who is on the floor yelling, screaming, and kicking? We, like the little kid, think if we yell and scream loud enough and long enough, we will eventually get what we want. What we do not understand is the same thing the little kid does not understand, we are hurting ourselves.

You may not see yourself as a brat in your relationship with God, but I can see that in my relationship with Him. Many times I have said, "Okay, God, now I am going to pray and do this novena. At the end of this novena, give it to me. It says right here in the book, nine times... Maybe you did not hear me God, so I will do it one more time... This is eighteen times now, God... Okay God, one more time and that is the last time, then are You going to get it because I am not going to speak to You anymore." Perhaps you have said, or heard someone else say, "I don't go to church anymore because Father so-and-so did something to me and I'm never stepping foot inside his church again." or "Why is God doing this to me? I'm good; in fact I'm great. Why isn't He doing what I want Him to do? He better do it now or I'm not going to speak to Him anymore." These are examples of spiritual temper tantrums.

When we act like brats we look at everyone else as the enemy, in competition with us. People have said to me, "Well, you know, this is a dog-eat-dog world, Father, and you just don't understand. I mean, come on, this is fine for church, but I live in the world out there." That is an excuse. I am a priest and unfortunately priests have their own little sub-culture of climbing to the top. It is just as much a dog-eat-dog world for me, as it is for you in many ways. Even worse, I have been told "I just have to be me, Father." I do not even know who *me* is yet, honestly, do you?! What you and I have in common when we act and talk like brats is our priorities are out of order. God is not the center of our lives, somebody else or something else is.

If we would be true children instead of brats, life would really go much better for us. It is not that when we act like brats God does not love us, when we act like brats we do not love ourselves. When we do not love ourselves, we obviously cannot love God. Therefore we continue to be brats spiritually which could lead to Atheism or to blaming God, saying to Him, "Look at all this war, all these babies dying. Look at all this pollution. Why are you doing this God, why are you allowing this evil to happen?" God then replies, "Wait a minute, why are *you* allowing this evil? I made a beautiful world. I gave you a beautiful sky and a beautiful earth, I gave you beautiful water; *you* are the ones polluting the earth. I made people out of love; *you* are the ones who are killing each other. I gave you enough, and here you are thinking you never have enough. Do not blame *Me* for something *you* should be taking care of."

Why do we allow it? Each one of us allows it. We cannot point the finger at anyone else. However, before we feel too guilty, we need to know God is aware we make mistakes. He is with us. He is the answer. Accepting blame is never easy. If you have children, how many times have you said to them, "That is not my responsibility, it is yours."? When we act like brats we do not accept responsibility or blame for anything, or we believe the world revolves around us and owes us a living. When we come to the realization that no one owes us anything, we go into fits of depression and spend thousands of dollars on psychiatrists in order to get our act together. We need to wake up and realize we are never going to get our act together. We can, however, let God handle our act for us; He has it together. Our Lady asks us to change from acting like brats, to acting like true children, placing our trust in the Lord. That change happens during the conversion of our hearts.

The change from brat to child, and the conversion of heart, does not happen overnight. It is a process, one that is helped by the Sacraments of the Church: the Eucharist and the Sacrament of Reconciliation. All we need to do is say, "Yes, God." Honestly, it is that simple. Unfortunately, it is never easy. We complicate it so much. Let us start with today, just today, and try to be children. Each time we come to Mass and receive the Lord in the Eucharist, when He is placed into our hand or mouth, pray, "Lord, thank You for making me Your child. Help me truly to be a child." He will answer that prayer because He wants us to be loving children.

How long has it been since you have been to the Sacrament of Reconciliation? That is too long. Your memory is not that good and you, like everyone else, block out what you do not want to remember. Receiving this Sacrament is like taking a personal inventory of your Spirit. It is asking in what areas of your life have you responded to God and what areas are causing you pain, what are you really sorry for having done and where are you really in need of God's healing and forgiveness. If you only receive the Sacrament of Reconciliation once in a blue moon, then you deaden your Spirit. By inviting God to be with you, to help you see where you need healing, you are shown the source and not the symptoms of your pain.

Let me give you an example. If the symptom is verbal profanity, then the source is anger and disrespect. Another symptom that is often overlooked is sexual sins; masturbation, premarital sex, adultery. These are symptoms and their source is lack of self-love. We need to present to God the sources of our sinfulness, not the symptoms. I believe we are misusing the Sacrament of Reconciliation by constantly presenting the symptoms alone to God. No wonder we repeatedly confess the same things. It is like a person whose arm is hanging off who says, "Oh that, I'll just put a Band-Aid on that—a little Neosporin and it will be fine." That is taking care of a symptom. When we are afraid to take care of the source, we die spiritually.

Sources take a lot more thought and prayer to discover than symptoms. Sure, most likely you have not killed anyone, but when was the last time you sliced someone to death with your tongue? If you are married, you may not have committed adultery, but have you been a loving spouse? See how that works? When you get so jaded and boxed in that there is no joy in the journey any longer, it becomes the same old boring stuff. Your relationships are falling apart and life becomes an endurance test. There is hope though. God always offers you another chance, Reconciliation is one of the chances He gives you. Do you give Him the chance to heal the sources of your sinfulness, to get in there and make you well again? Do you allow Him to truly make you His child again?

You may say, "I don't want to go to Reconciliation. God can forgive me. I don't have to go to a priest. I can just tell God." Yes, you can, but you probably do not because even in private you do not want to admit to God you are less than perfect. The Lord knows that because we are human we need other human beings to help us, so He gave us priests. Priests are there to give a human touch. It is God who forgives, the priest is His instrument. God can forgive without using a priest, however by going to a priest in the Sacrament of Reconciliation, what you are saying is you are sorry enough that you want to publicly ask for help and receive assurance that your sin is forgiven. Reconciliation is the celebration of God's forgiveness and acceptance of His help. Through Reconciliation you are made holy again.

How many times does God have to show us all He wants to do is love us? All He wants to do is take us in His hands, as He said throughout the Old Testament and the New Testament. Jesus tells us to pray saying Abba, Father, daddy, papa. That is how close God wants to be with us. Yet we continue to be brats. When will we understand? When will we realize we are the ones preventing God from being close to us? We are the ones who hold Him at an arms distance. We are the ones saying, "No, I really can't because I'm not worthy." Of course we are not worthy to approach God, we are sinners. Fortunately *'worthy'* does not hold any weight at all with God. What does carry weight is *'willing.'* Are we willing?

That is what Jesus asks, not "Are you worthy?" but "Are you willing to say 'yes'?" That is all He needs, just your 'yes.' It is not easy, but it is simple. Being a child of God is not easy, but it is simple, because being a child of God is simply saying, "Yes, God, I do believe You love me. I believe You sent Your Son to die for me. You loved Him so much and you love me so much that You raised Him from death, I believe that. To this day, I believe You constantly send people, little angels, into my life to call me home; to love me and give me what I truly need, not necessarily what I want, but what I truly need. Dear Father, I do believe that." He has it together. All we need to do is say "yes."

Unfortunately, because it is not easy, we do not like to be true children of God. We want to take control. A brat always has to be in control. A child is completely at the disposal of its' parents. A true child is simply there, trusting to be taken care of, fed, nurtured, cherished and loved. It is no wonder some people have such a problem being children of God when they destroy their own children. It is a tragedy. Millions of children are killed before they are even born, and so many who are allowed to live are not allowed to be children.

From the very beginning of life, children in America are seated in front of a television. What priorities are taught to them when they are given Nintendo and told they have to be the best to get ahead? Children are starved for love and affection and never allowed to just waste time. They are starved for somebody to really nurture them, to allow them to be children.

If we do not allow our children to be children, then how can we expect to be children? We should allow our children to waste time occasionally. Forget the piano lesson, ballet lesson, soccer, football and basketball practice. Forget about rushing around frantically. Forget the chaos. Chaos and confusion come from the devil, not from God. We need to slow down and put God back into the center of our lives. When we are anxious, worried, angry or wanting to control the situations around us, that is an indication God is not in the center of our lives. When He is, nothing changes outside, but everything changes inside. We can deal with the most difficult situations and still be very much at peace. People can come up and yell at us and we can say, "Well, okay, I'll listen and think about it," instead of screaming back at them.

When was the last time you asked the Lord, "Lord, who am I? Please tell me." If you do that, He will tell you, "My dear one, you are a child of God." Wow, talk about an identity! When you allow God to be as really present to you as He wants to be, then you take Him with you everywhere you go and you begin to see Him in everyone. What a difference it would be to our world if you and I, who are Catholic and who have the Lord really present to us in the Sacrament of Eucharist, would be really present to Him and to each other. When God is at the center of our hearts, there is peace and mercy there. It is then we act like, and truly are, children of God.

EPILOGUE

At whatever point in this journey back to God Our Father, which each of us is on, it is truly a gift to know we are not alone. Not only is Jesus walking with us in His Holy Spirit, accompanied by Our Lady and the angels and saints (we are stumbling all over them and do not even know it!), but we also have each other in the community which Jesus gave us—the Church.

When we are tempted to give up hope, when the darkness comes and we believe we are all alone, that is when we must reach out to the community. We cannot make the journey alone, it would be impossible and unbearable, which is why Jesus gave us each other. This is the reason we need to reflect often on the words of St. Paul to the Philippians and make them our own:

"I give thanks to my God at every remembrance of you, praying always with joy in my every prayer for all of you, because of your partnership for the gospel from the first day until now. I am confident of this, that the one who began a good work in you will continue to complete it until the day of Christ Jesus. It is right that I should think this way about all of you, because I hold you in my heart, you who are all partners with me in grace, both in my imprisonment and in the defense and confirmation of the gospel.

For God is my witness, how I long for all of you with the affection of Christ Jesus. And this is my prayer: that your love may increase ever more and more in knowledge and every kind of perception, to discern what is of value, so that you may be pure and blameless for the day of Christ, filled with the fruit of righteousness that comes through Jesus Christ for the glory and praise of God." *(Phil 1:3-11)*

This is truly Hope for the Journey!